the

MR. X INTERVIEWS

Volume 1

WORLD VIEWS FROM A
FICTIONAL US SOVEREIGN CREDITOR

LUKE GROMEN

AVIVA
PUBLISHING
New York

The Mr. X Interviews, Volume 1: World Views from a Fictional US Sovereign Creditor

Published by:
Aviva Publishing
Lake Placid, NY
(518) 523-1320
www.AvivaPubs.com

Address all inquiries to:
Luke Gromen
info@fftt-llc.com
440-732-0764
www.FFTT-LLC.com

ISBN: 978-1-947937-10-9

Library of Congress Control Number: 2018912681

Editor: Tyler Tichelaar/Superior Book Productions
Design & Layout: Birte Kahrs

Every attempt has been made to source all quotes properly.
First Edition

TO MY WIFE:

None of any of this could have ever happened without you, using the broadest definition possible of the word "this." Thank you.

TO MY SONS:

Always remember the world is not black and white, but countless shades of gray. Try to understand as many of the perspectives of the shades of gray as you can—it will make both you and the world a better place. I hope I have taught you as much as each of you have taught me.

CONTENTS

ACKNOWLEDGMENTS

Learning about the global currency system from both a "flows" and "realpolitik" perspective requires standing on the shoulders of giants, including historical figures, friends, and people using pseudonyms: Jacques Rueff, Felix Somary, Dimitri Chalvatsiotis (more widely-known as DC), Kirk McKeown, Grant Williams, Tom McNamara, Peter Truszkowski, "Another," FOA, FOFOA, and many others. If I have not listed you here by name, please do not take my omission as intentional or a devaluing of your contribution to my education. I am indebted to you all.

DISCLOSURES

officers, employees, or members of their families might, from time to time, have financial interests with affiliates of companies whose securities have been discussed in this publication.

PREFACE

Inspiration for this book came from one of my best friends on Wall Street. He thought it might be helpful to our customers if I conducted a mock interview with a fictional head of a foreign sovereign creditor of the US using the Socratic method.

This construct would allow me to elucidate some of the thought processes and events we had been describing in our work and observing in markets regarding what increasingly appeared to me to be monumental changes developing in the global economy and global financial system. This format also allowed me to hypothesize some of the potential reasoning behind those events.

While I was unsure of how the finished report would be received, I was pleasantly surprised—customers loved the format and began to ask for more "Mr. X" interviews.

What follows is a collection of some of the early "Mr. X" interviews, combined with some new interviews I have "conducted."

Without further ado, my interview with "Mr. X."

LUKE GROMEN

INTRODUCTION

Somebody once said, "Events can go from impossible to inevitable without ever stopping at improbable."

I first met Mr. X at an investment conference social gathering at the Ritz Carlton in Grand Cayman. Typically, the conversation at such events is topical and brief, but he and I hit it off immediately despite a nearly forty-year difference in our ages. The discussion centered on what to my eyes appeared to be a rapidly-accelerating shift in the way the world's currency and economic system had functioned for the past half-century. As such, I was pleasantly surprised when Mr. X reached out to me some months later.

He said we needed to sit down to talk, and in an accent that was difficult to place, noted that it was "somewhat urgent." He told me he would be in New York on short notice in two days' time and asked whether I could meet him while he was in the city. Intrigued, I told him I would be happy to and immediately made the necessary arrangements to fly to New York from my home in Cleveland.

After touching down in the rain at LaGuardia, I made my way to the luggage claim area where I was surprised to find a driver holding a placard with my last name on it. I approached him, shook his hand, and he led me to the car. The car made its way through the grim weather into midtown Manhattan, arriving an hour later at the restaurant where I was to meet Mr. X.

I opened my umbrella as I exited the sedan, grabbed my bag, and headed into the restaurant. As I shook the light rain off my umbrella by the door, the maître d' asked, "Mr. Gromen?" I smiled, nodded, and was escorted to a small private room in the back of the restaurant.

Inside sat a distinguished-looking older gentleman. He rose as I entered, extended his hand, and said, "Luke, so good to see you. I trust your travels were good?"

"They were," I replied. "Thank you for arranging the sedan. It was totally unexpected and unnecessary, but greatly appreciated!"

"You are welcome," he replied. "I appreciate you coming to New York on such short notice, so I thought it might be a nice gesture."

"It most definitely was. I have to say, I was surprised to hear from you; pleasantly so, but surprised nonetheless…and I must say, I'm more than a little curious."

Mr. X smiled appreciatively. "I imagine you are curious! I reached out to you because in my travels, few people I have talked to have the ability to put the pieces together like you seem able to do, at least based on our conversation over drinks a few months ago."

"Thank you—coming from you, that's very flattering," I replied.

"However, I did not ask you to meet me here to flatter you. I came here to tell you that the trends you began describing to me over drinks—you are correct about them…far more correct than you possibly know."

A touch of excitement started at the pit of my stomach and bubbled upward, manifesting as an uncontainable grin…. "Really?" I said incredulously.

"Yes," Mr. X replied. "In fact, the trends are playing out far more quickly than even you thought possible. The pace at which the USD-centric global monetary system is breaking down is accelerating dramatically."

Chapter 1

THE FIRST MEETING, DINNER, JANUARY 2016

THE DOLLAR CENTRIC SYSTEM IS BREAKING DOWN

My conversation with Mr. X became all the more intriguing and intense after that sentence. For the remainder of this book, I will share with you the transcript of that conversation and the conversations that followed. I asked his permission to record it with my digital voice recorder so I could convey it to you accurately; it was so important that I did not want to miss a single word, plus his intention is for me to share this information with the world by writing a series of reports.

My firm, "Forest for the Trees," or FFTT for short, is an investment research firm that occupies a unique niche on Wall Street, putting together a variety of publicly-available datapoints in an unconventional manner to identify developing investment trends.

I had previously told Mr. X that I wanted to write a book on the changes we were seeing in the global currency system, although I never suspected at the time he would give me much of the material I needed.

Luke: When you say the USD-centric global monetary system is breaking down, what do you mean?

Mr. X: At the highest levels of global finance, it has long been known that the number-one problem in global economics is the dollar-centric system. In other words, that there would eventually be a dollar crisis.

Luke: I assume that when you refer to the " USD-centric system," you are referring to what is sometimes called the petrodollar system?

Mr. X: Yes, exactly. Let me preface this statement by saying I love the United States. I maintain a residence here in New York, and I have met countless wonderful Americans, many of whom I count among my dearest friends. The US is one of the greatest nations on the planet....

Luke: I feel a "but" coming on.

Mr. X: (Smiling) Yes…and here it is: But I have always been surprised how little most US citizens, and investment professionals specifically, understand that much of the style and standard of living that most US citizens have grown accustomed to is a function of the petrodollar system.

As you know, under the petrodollar from 1973 until about mid-2014, oil was only priced in USD globally. When oil prices got too low, oil exporters like OPEC and Russia found their budgets under pressure and burned down FX reserves, so it usually fell to Saudi Arabia as the world's swing producer to cut oil production and stabilize oil prices.

On the flip side, from 1973 until about three years ago, when oil prices got too high, the US Fed began raising rates to slow down the US economy (which was also the world's biggest economy and energy importer) to bring oil prices back into an acceptable range.

There has been much discussion about this "petrodollar system," but in the end, I would say the non-US world tolerated it. The world worked. Your Fed chairman Paul Volcker, in particular, earned the petrodollar system a tremendous amount of credibility in 1979-1981 when he showed he was willing to put the US economy into tremendous distress by raising rates into a vicious US recession to fight rising oil price inflation. He showed a commitment to keep the USD "as good as gold" for oil, even though the United States had defaulted on its gold commitments to its creditors like my nation only eight years before.

Luke: So if that was the dollar-centric system, as you called it, what has changed with it and what leads you to believe a dollar crisis is coming?

Mr. X: I believe a dollar crisis is coming because of the clues being given off by the global oil market. In the last two to three years, some very significant changes in the oil market have happened based on moves made by both major global oil importers and exporters. Perhaps the most recent one came at the end of 2015, when your US Congress repealed the forty-year-old US crude oil export ban.

Tell me, why would the US ever export crude oil for dollars when from 1973-2014, the US could simply print dollars for ever-growing amounts of imported oil? That makes no sense using "the old lens."

Luke: That's a great point; it doesn't make any sense. That is something I've written about a number of times. What are some other clues you are referring to?

5

Mr. X: Well, the clues started in earnest in the fall of 2014, when Saudi Arabia led OPEC in declining to support USD oil prices and continued to run production at high levels—that was a very different direction from OPEC's actions the prior thirty or more years during prior occasions when the price of oil had fallen sharply.

[Here, Mr. X paused to reach into his bag to retrieve a news article he had printed out.] OPEC (Organization of Oil Exporting Countries) then emphatically reinforced its fall 2014 decision with this announcement in December 2015 in which OPEC officials explicitly stated that "If the Russians and Americans have no production limits, we will not enforce them either. This, in effect, amounted to a statement by OPEC that "We would rather maximize oil production and dis-hoard US Treasury bonds (USTs)/USDs than maximize oil prices and hoard USTs/USDs."

Of course, all I read in the Western mainstream financial media in the aftermath of that 2014 OPEC decision and the ensuing drop in oil prices was how screwed Saudi Arabia was because of how rapidly it was burning down its USD reserves, which made me laugh out loud; in my opinion, the Western mainstream financial media doesn't get it.

Luke: Why did the Western media's assessment of the Saudi position post-OPEC meeting make you laugh?

Mr. X: Because the Western media writes as if the USD is the center of the world.

Luke: Well, it is, isn't it? The Western financial media has a point, doesn't it? I mean, don't the Saudis have USD-denominated debt and extensive social obligations?

Mr. X: Oh sure, but let me ask you: What nation would not lend to Saudi or supply Saudi's social needs in exchange for the right to price Saudi oil in its own currency? Do you think *any* nation would decline that offer?

This is why the Western mainstream financial media makes me laugh. It thinks the US dollar is the real value rather than the Saudi oil that has effectively backed those dollars for forty years. The same dollar that the Fed was not so long ago printing $85B per month of out of thin air!

For those who think the dollar is the real value, I would challenge them—next time you need to fill up your car, why don't you take it to your local Fed branch, fill it up with dollars, and see how far it takes you? Westerners have become so accustomed to the USD effectively equaling oil that they have forgotten it is oil that is the real value, not the USD.

Luke, you have kids, right? Have you watched the Harry Potter movie series with them? What is it they say in Harry Potter? "The wand chooses the wizard, not the other way around"? Well, most Americans seem to have forgotten that it is oil that chose the dollar as the world's monopoly reserve currency for oil, not the other way around.

And just as Americans have forgotten that it is oil that chose the USD as reserve, your American politicians have forgotten that if oil chose the USD as the world's oil monopoly reserve currency, there is no theoretical reason why oil could not "un-choose" the USD.

Luke: I understand that (and I agree with you), but I've had people respond in the past that if the Saudis did that, wouldn't the US just invade Saudi and take over the oil fields?

Mr. X: A very American response indeed! I suppose the US could make such a move were Saudi to "un-choose" the dollar as the world's oil monopoly currency, but let me ask you as before—do you think no other nation would be willing to move its army to Saudi Arabia's aid for the promise of future Saudi oil priced in its own currency? China perhaps?

Let me assure you: Any nation with an army would be willing to move to Saudi Arabia's aid for the promise of future cheap Saudi oil…and even a nation without an army might be willing to help out; heaven knows the Russians would be happy to sell them the weapons!

Luke: Good point. Let's move back to a less grim topic and further discuss the major change in the global oil market you mentioned. Are there other clues about this major change? If so, what are they?

Mr. X: Yes. In addition to the change in the way the US and OPEC have acted in the past three years versus the prior forty years, global oil exporters and commodity producers have "flipped the script," if you will, by de-pegging from or devaluing the USD. Russia, Kazakhstan, Iran, Nigeria, Angola, Azerbaijan, Venezuela, Argentina, South Africa, Angola—that's a lot of countries all choosing to do effectively the same thing:

Rather than burning FX reserves down and then devaluing their currency, they have shown a willingness to de-peg earlier on and take the inflationary pain to their economies.

Luke: What do you think accounts for their change in behavior on that front?

Mr. X: The answer to that question is also the final clue that something big has changed in the global oil market. I think it is at least partially because the world's new biggest oil importer, China, is willing to pay for oil in Chinese yuan instead of dollars and then offer a credible physical gold settlement of any offshore yuan net balances created by selling oil in yuan.

Luke: Pricing oil in yuan? Hasn't selling or buying oil in any currency that is not dollars historically been a big geopolitical no-no? To ask more directly, didn't changing the pricing of his oil to euros contribute to Saddam's downfall?

Mr. X: That is generally not something talked about in polite company.

Luke: Well, lucky for you, I'm from Cleveland.

Mr. X: [laughing] In that case, it would seem to strain credulity to believe that Saddam's move to switch oil pricing from USD to EUR in the fall of 2000 had absolutely nothing to do with his fate. Interestingly, recently-released Hillary Clinton emails suggest that oil pricing currency issues may have also been a contributing factor in Qaddafi's downfall in Libya in 2011.

Luke: Chalk one up for the "conspiracy theory" crowd, perhaps.

Mr. X: Indeed.

Luke: So if that is the case, and Russia and Iran began selling oil to China in yuan instead of dollars, why hasn't the United States reacted?

Mr. X: What makes you say the United States hasn't reacted? Since shortly before or shortly after the so-called "Holy Grail" energy deals were discussed and signed between Russia and China in May 2014 (that were later shown to be yuan oil deals), there has been a spontaneous outbreak of open war in Russia's client state Syria, a color revolution in Ukraine, sanctions on Russia and Iran, and heightened tensions with China.... That strikes me as quite an incredible string of coincidences.

[Smiling] Perhaps your American media has convinced the American public to believe those geopolitical events were all mere coincidences, but please tell me that you do not ascribe all of those events to mere coincidence, Luke....

Luke: No, no, I don't unfortunately...and your point is well-taken. Let us return to your original point about Chinese Yuan (CNY) oil pricing: Why would any oil exporter like Russia or Iran agree to take CNY instead of USD for its oil?

Mr. X: The easy answer is that China is now many of these nation's biggest customer, and these nations need Chinese goods for their people.

The more nuanced answer is China is offering credible physical gold settlement, which then gives both China and these oil exporters the ability to get away from the USD that over the past fifteen years the United States has increasingly been using as a weapon against any nation that disagrees with Washington's political agenda.

By way of background on the "weaponization" of the USD:

By the mid-2000s, the USD was the only thing the world really needed the US for on a net basis anymore (besides certain defense and technology products). Given this, the US government decided the USD was an effective foreign policy tool. As noted by former senior US Treasury official Juan Zarate in his 2013 book *Treasury's War*:

> The dollar serves as the global reserve currency and the currency of choice for international trade, and New York has remained a core financial capital and hub for dollar-clearing transactions. *With this concentration of financial and commercial power comes the ability to wield access to American markets, American banks, and American dollars as financial weapons.*

> Treasury's power ultimately stems from the ability of the US to use its financial powers with global effect. This ability, in turn, stems from the centrality and stability of New York as a global financial center, the importance of the USD as a reserve currency, and the demonstration effects, regulatory or otherwise, taken by the US in the broader international system. *If the US economy loses its predominance, or the USD sufficiently weakens, our ability to wage financial warfare could wane.* [Emphasis mine]

Luke: What do you mean by "credible physical gold settlement"?

Mr. X: [Reaching into his briefcase and pulling out another piece of paper] Look at this article: In 2015, the NY COMEX gold exchange settled less than fifty tons of physical gold all year. In contrast, on average the Shanghai Gold Exchange settled over fifty tons of physical gold every single week of 2015. If you want physical gold, which exchange is more credible?

Luke: Why the difference between paper gold and physical gold?

Mr. X: Paper gold is, in extremis, merely an obligation of a Too-Big-To-Fail (TBTF) bullion bank, which was shown in 2008 to be an obligation of the US government in extremis. In other words, paper gold = USDs. If you are going to take paper gold as trade settlement, you might as well just stick with USTs.

Luke: Got it. So when I put all of your clues together, from the US exporting oil, to OPEC no longer limiting production to support USD oil prices, to other oil exporters de-pegging from USD, to China pricing oil in CNY and settling balances in physical gold, I am left with a string of compelling clues but no overriding theme to connect them. What am I missing? Why are these things happening?

[Here Mr. X took out the chart below to show me.]

Mr. X: To see what is happening through the "oil balance of payments lens" I referenced earlier, you must put yourself in my shoes, or Russia's shoes, or Saudi's shoes, or China's shoes. From 1973 until about 2000, the United States managed the USD responsibly for the benefit of all in the world, including creditors. Even when it required Paul Volcker taking rates to the teens and crushing the domestic economy, America managed the USD to be "as good as gold for oil."

If you look at a chart of US Fed Funds Rates v. oil prices, this relationship is pretty obvious between 1973 and 2000 (note "EMs" in chart = Emerging Markets).

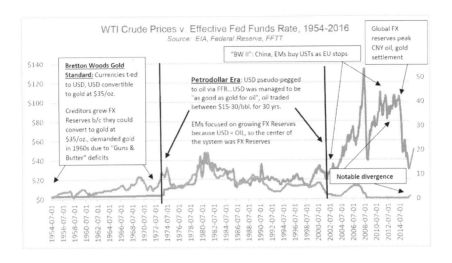

WTI Crude Prices v. Effective Fed Funds Rate, 1954-2016
Source: EIA, Federal Reserve, FFTT

Luke: So then what happened in 2000?

Mr. X: The USD became a victim of its own success in a way. The moves Volcker made in the early 1980s established a fertile breeding ground for financialization of the US economy during a time of rapid financial innovation. The net of it was that by 2000, the US economy had become too financialized to withstand much more than a token rate hike, as evidenced by how badly the US tech bubble blew up in 2000.

Not long after the tech bubble blew up, the historically-unique combination of geological realities that began developing in the global oil patch (rising oil discovery and production) cost curves, and rapidly-growing Emerging Markets (EMs) led to a sharp rise in the price of oil. Under the petrodollar system, that should have required the Fed to raise rates to keep the price of oil relatively steady in USD terms, but the Fed did not do so.

Luke: But they didn't because they were afraid of popping the housing bubble.

Mr. X: Perhaps that was the reason, but regardless, the Fed didn't raise rates like it should have. That much can be seen in the chart I just showed you.

Luke: So why didn't the world move to ditch the USD in global oil trade at that point, if the US wasn't holding up its end of the "petrodollar system" bargain?

Mr. X: Well, for some nations, seeing what happened to Saddam may have been motivation enough. Others, like Russia and much of Southeast Asia, were still recovering from their own EM crises that occurred in the mid to late 1990s.

And China probably didn't do anything because by virtue of getting into the WTO in late 2001, the Americans essentially began trading large remaining chunks of the US industrial base for steady Chinese purchases of USTs, which was something the Americans desperately needed after the formation of the EUR because the Europeans basically stopped incrementally funding the US government (buying USTs) after the EUR's launch in 1999. China was getting a great deal—the staggering number of US IOUs (US Treasury bonds) they bought were essentially being collateralized immediately by US production capacity with ready contracts to sell back to the US.

Luke: Wow...I never thought of it that way. Washington essentially pawned large remaining chunks of the US' industrial base in exchange for a UST buyer willing to fund Washington's largesse for just a little longer?

Mr. X: It's sobering when you think of it that way, isn't it? But you have to remember that these aren't the only reasons the world didn't try to ditch the USD for oil trade in the early 2000s when the

US started to fail at keeping its end of the bargain to manage the dollar for the good of the world.

You must remember the zeitgeist of the times: Everyone knew the US financial system was the strongest in the world, the envy of the world. The world abided by the "Washington Consensus" and the neoliberal economic values it espoused. [He reached into his folder to pull out another chart to show me.]

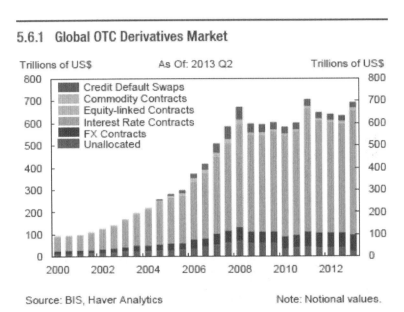

5.6.1 Global OTC Derivatives Market

Source: BIS, Haver Analytics   Note: Notional values.

And so beginning around 2000 or so, when the American and global banks began offering us these new "interest rate derivatives" that allowed us to hedge our exposure to rising interest rates that rising oil prices would normally have portended, without having to sell our USTs, why would we have ever questioned them? They were the smartest guys in the room. The strongest system on the planet.

Luke: So their pitch to you was "Don't sell your USTs due to higher oil prices like you might have done in the past; buy an interest rate swap from us instead that will hedge your risk, and we will make you whole if rates rise."

Mr. X: Effectively…and judging by the growth in notional (face) value of interest rate swaps and other credit derivatives from 2000 through the 2008 crisis, many investors and creditors appear to have believed their pitch. According to the Bank for International Settlements (BIS), the notional value of interest rate derivatives outstanding alone rose from around $50 trillion in 2000 to nearly $500 trillion by 2008.

Luke: Holy cow! So you're saying interest rate derivatives, which are essentially just insurance policies designed to protect bondholders from losses in case interest rates rise, rose from $50 trillion in face value insurance policies in 2000 to $500 trillion in face value insurance policies by 2008?

Mr. X: Yes. The face value of "interest rate insurance policies" outstanding rose from around 1x global GDP in 2000 to 8-9x global GDP in the span of eight years.

Luke: And you believed that the "underwriters" of these "interest rate insurance policies," called interest rate derivatives, would make good on these policies? Or, at least you *did* until 2008, when the US and global financial system imploded?

Mr. X: Yes. You have to remember that the Washington Consensus and neoliberal economics had decades of proof of success behind it. The vaunted American financial system was the strongest in the world.

Luke: And then in the span of a few months, the vaunted US financial system was revealed to be made out of little more than "balsa wood and baby tears," to borrow a phrase from then *Daily Show* host and comedian Jon Stewart.

Mr. X: Yes. Our first concern was acting with our partners in other nations around the world and in the United States to prevent a total systemic collapse…and let me tell you, that was much closer than most would care to admit! However, once the system was stabilized, there began to be grumbling around the world as US creditors all came to the realization that something needed to change with the system.

The reality is that the rest of the world knew the system would fail someday. We had known for a long time. BIS Chair Jelle Zijlstra was a brilliant man—let me read to you what he describes here about the "the 3rd Oil Crisis" he saw coming as early as 1980, understanding that he wrote this *long before* that crisis occurred in 2008:

> [T]he 2nd Oil Crisis could be worked through, slowly, but the international financial system could not survive a 3rd Oil Crisis—the inflation would make it impossible to recycle the petrodollars to the oil importing countries with any hope of repayment, trade would crumble, and the system would be brought to its knees."

Luke: Interesting…did Zijlstra also offer a prescription for a fix by any chance?

Mr. X: As I said, Zijlstra was a brilliant man, so naturally he did offer such a prescription in 1981, when he described the breakdown of the USD-centric Bretton Woods system that had occurred two decades prior:

> [T]he 1960s saw a growing disequilibrium in international payments, consequent on the deficit in the US balance of payments. The dollar became overvalued and the US found it increasingly difficult to meet its obligations to convert the dollar (into gold.) *It is my firm conviction that a devaluation of the dollar combined with a substantial increase in the price of gold (as provided for in Article IV of the then Articles of Agreement of the International Monetary Fund) would have meant a real improvement of the situation.* [Emphasis mine]

Luke: Okay, so, in light of what Zijlstra said so long ago and what happened in 2008, you mentioned once the system was stabilized, there was grumbling internationally about the system. What did that grumbling say? What needed to change?

Mr. X: Not too long after the 2008 crisis, I was visiting the United States when I saw a protestor on TV somewhere holding a sign that said, "No more capitalism for the poor and socialism for the rich." I doubt that protestor realized it, but that sentiment was being echoed with the world's creditor nations, many of which were Emerging Markets.

Judging by the triumphalism in US financial media about the Fed's role in saving the financial system, the Washington Consensus and neoliberal economists don't seem to realize it, but their policies were totally discredited after 2008.

Luke: Why?

Mr. X: Because the policies they implemented in the United States in response to the crisis were nothing in severity like those implemented in Russia in the mid-1990s, in Southeast Asia in the late 1990s, or in Argentina in the early 2000s. It was, like the protestor's sign said, "Capitalism for the poor (EM/creditor economies) and socialism for the rich (the US economy.)" That caught creditor nations' attention; we knew we needed the system to change.

Luke: Change in what way? And does that change relate to the oil market change we discussed earlier, and if so, how?

Mr. X: Very good question! Yes, it relates to the oil market change; in fact, it has everything to do with the oil market change *because the oil market is being used to force the change!*

Luke: As if I weren't intrigued enough already! Please elaborate.

Mr. X: For a deceptively simple reason: Under the petrodollar system, one of the biggest drivers of global balance-of-payment imbalances has always been the oil market.

To oversimplify, the petrodollar system meant that the Americans got 10-15 percent of the world's oil for free, every single day, and in return, the Emerging Markets got US production capabilities, access to US consumer markets (into which EMs indirectly supplied the lending capital), and a great big pile of US Treasury bonds.

There are those who say US creditor nations stockpiled USTs as a way of keeping their currency weak relative to the USD to remain competitive, but that doesn't matter for purposes of this discussion because it, too, hints at the same long-standing imbalance being remedied through the oil market. As proof, now that oil is at $27 as we talk here today in January 2016, those EMs sure are selling those USTs rapidly, are they not?

Luke: Okay, so then what is the critical change in the global oil market hinted at by the clues we discussed earlier?

Mr. X: Remember what Zijlstra said. Sometime after 2008, the world realized it could no longer afford to give the US 10-15 percent of the world's oil for free every single day because everyone realized it had become impossible to recycle the petrodollars back to US debtors with any hope of repayment in real (oil) terms. Right around the same time, the US began to realize the petrodollar, its "exorbitant privilege," had become more of a burden than a privilege.

Luke: Given what happened in 2008, I can understand why the world would realize it could no longer afford to give the US 10-15 percent of the world's oil for free every single day, but why do you say the US realized the exorbitant privilege had become a burden?

Mr. X: Oh, there have been numerous clues. Joe Biden's chief economist Jared Bernstein wrote an op-ed to that effect in the third quarter of 2014 in *The New York Times* entitled "Dethrone King Dollar." Larry Summers wrote and spoke numerous times right around that same time that it was critical the United States begin exporting oil. Consummate insiders like that do not speak out of turn. Have you ever read what Senator Elizabeth Warren said Larry Summers told her about being a Washington insider? I have it here with me.

[Mr. X reached into his folder file and then pulled out a sheet of paper that he read aloud.]

Larry leaned back in his chair and offered me some advice.... He teed it up this way: I had a choice. I could be an insider or I could be an outsider. Outsiders can say whatever they want. But people on the inside don't listen to them. Insiders, however, get lots of access and a chance to push their ideas. People—powerful people—listen to what they have to say. But insiders also understand one unbreakable rule: Don't criticize other insiders.

I had been warned.

[Source: https://www.washingtonpost.com/news/wonk/wp/2014/12/14/elizabeth-warren-is-changing-washington-without-giving-up-her-outside-status/]

Luke: Having heard Senator Warren's quote, I don't disagree with your point about Summers and Jared Bernstein's op-eds.

Mr. X: So do you see what is happening in the oil markets yet, through the "oil balance-of-payments lens"?

Luke: At the risk of sounding thick to you, I don't. I apologize, but could you lay it out more explicitly?

Mr. X: You are not thick at all my friend, and I'd be happy to be more explicit. It is very straightforward:

The USD will no longer enjoy the monopoly on oil pricing and settlement it has enjoyed for the past forty-three years. Oil will begin to be priced in multiple currencies, likely including CNY and EUR.

This then means that no one will be allowed to write IOUs he never has to cash and can always roll over for oil any longer, as the

US did for the past forty-three years under the petrodollar system. Going forward, any net trade imbalances caused by oil will be able to be settled in a neutral settlement asset—perhaps physical gold, perhaps IMF SDRs, perhaps some combination of the two—and that neutral reserve asset will float in every currency in local currency terms so that energy creditor purchasing power can be maintained in oil terms, unlike what the US has done since 2000 with USTs (but tried to fake like it is still doing so with interest rate derivatives from 2000-2008.)

Luke: Why gold or some other "neutral reserve asset"?

Mr. X: Because only a few currencies are big enough to be "global oil currencies"—aside from the USD, only the EUR and CNY. And neither the Germans nor the Chinese are willing to pay the price needed to become the world's sole global oil currency, which they learned from watching the Americans. So if the EUR and CNY do not want to become the new sole oil currencies, then a neutral reserve asset must be chosen.

Luke: But the SDR market or the physical gold market are nowhere near big enough to handle the physical oil market....

Mr. X: No, they are not. *But the new neutral settlement asset will be made "big enough"—in fact, that is what is happening in oil markets right now.* Let's just use "gold" for ease and sake of discussion. If gold is to be the new neutral asset for settling oil transactions, then gold needs to be made much bigger relative to oil (and relative to all other global assets).

But since roughly the second quarter of 2013, somebody, for some reason, has refused to allow record global physical gold demand to translate into record physical gold prices in USDs. While this "pegging" of USD/GOLD worked for a while, once Russia and

China began moving away from USD oil, if gold was the new oil settlement asset but it was not allowed to rise in USD (pegged to USD), then the only release valve was oil and the USD…*so the price of oil began collapsing as the USD skyrocketed due to its de facto gold peg.*

When Russia and China began settling oil in physical gold, the physical oil market was some 25x the size of the physical gold market. Today, the physical oil market is only 10x the size of the physical gold market…this has been reflected in the Gold/Oil ratio (GOR), which has risen from 13x in fall 2014 to 41x today, an all-time high.

Luke: So whoever is "pseudo-pegging" the USD to gold is effectively *forcing the oil market to get small enough to fit into the physical gold market* instead of allowing the physical gold market to get "big enough" to settle the physical oil market?

Mr. X: Yes! But this situation cannot persist for very long, not for very long at all!

Luke: Why not?

Mr. X: Because while, as Western financial media often notes, "gold isn't used for anything," oil is! And once China launches a CNY-denominated oil contract, whoever has been effectively capping the gold market will increasingly force the oil market to fit into the gold market! Those who have been laughing at the so-called "gold bugs" will cease laughing when the price of oil collapses to levels that make large percentages of the world's oil supplies uneconomic, most of all the highest cost producer in the world: US shale producers!

Perhaps "somebody" thinks he can cap the price of gold to maintain the hegemony of the USD, but there are more important things in the world than the USD's hegemony! Let me ask you: If a significant percentage of the world's oil production is uneconomic at current prices and, before too long, will go offline, what will happen to the global economy, to humanity?

Then "King Dollar" will have no kingdom to rule over, no? And with no kingdom, tell me again, what would back King Dollar?

Ironically, because gold is "not used for anything," it can be inflated as much as it needs to be in order to satisfy its role as the world's new oil reserve asset, and I believe it will be before too long because certain people do not wish to see what happens when a significant percentage of the world's oil production goes offline.

Luke: "Certain people?" Like whom?

Mr. X: People like the BIS, who, per Zijlstra's comments, knew this crisis was coming thirty-five years ago...or perhaps even China, which will soon have the ability to price physical oil and physical gold on its own in CNY, and which has said that suppliers may have to pay the local CNY gold fix price and that the CNY would be fully convertible under the CNY oil contract.

It could even be an oil nation. They all hold lots of gold reserves, right? What would happen to King Dollar if Russia or Saudi announced that it would now value physical gold at 1,000 barrels per ounce? The widely-trumpeted Saudi and Russian FX reserve "problems" would disappear quite rapidly, wouldn't they?

Washington thinks King Dollar has the last say in this game, but I think Washington's hubris has clouded its judgment.

Luke: Why couldn't Washington just raise rates again like Paul Volcker did to defend King Dollar, to make the USD "as good as gold for oil" again?

Mr. X: Oh, it could. But USD oil cost curves suggest rates would have to rise hundreds of basis points, not just 100 basis points…and every 100 basis-point hike is $180B in interest expense when you have $18 trillion in Federal debt as we sit here in January 2016…and $180 billion is some 6-8 percent of US Federal tax receipts in good times.

Furthermore, the $18 trillion figure ignores the fact that your government owes more than $100 trillion in entitlements to its citizens, and the Baby Boomer demographic has either already turned or will soon turn a number of these entitlement programs cash flow negative, which will necessitate a further acceleration in US Federal borrowing.

If you raised rates hundreds of basis points to make the USD "as good as gold for oil" again, US Federal interest expense would spike even as Federal tax receipts plummeted while the financialized US economy imploded. The math doesn't work, and even if it did, it is a moot point because the US economy is already not weathering its first 25 basis point (bp) hike in ten years very well.

Already, US mainstream economists are pushing the Fed to pause or reverse course…. They do not have the fortitude of your man Volcker…but then again, they can't. The US economy is very differently-structured and much more indebted now than it was then.

Luke: You said neither the Germans nor the Chinese are willing to "pay the price" needed to become the world's sole global oil currency, "which they learned from watching the Americans." Why not? What is the price?

Mr. X: Running ever-growing deficits and hollowing out your manufacturing and export infrastructure. In short, bankrupting your country in the long run for a debt-fueled consumption and government-spending boom in the relative near-term.

Luke: Ah, gotcha. Clearly neither the Germans nor the Chinese would want that to happen.

Mr. X: No, which is why they have structured their currencies the way they have. The EUR and CNY are ingeniously structured to be the diametric opposites of how the USD is structured.

Luke: What do you mean?

Mr. X: US Treasury Secretary John Connolly famously said, "The USD is our currency, but it's your problem." That's because after the gold window was closed, the dollar was backed by a promise to manage the USD to be as good as gold for oil. In other words, if gold prices start rising in USD terms, it's a sign to creditors that the USD is being mismanaged; that creditors are getting screwed. The USD gets weaker when gold rises. That's why Paul Volcker once said, "Gold is my enemy."

But gold really isn't the enemy...that's like blaming the thermometer for the temperature in Phoenix in the summertime. The enemy is unconstrained US government spending.

In contrast, the EUR and CNY mark their gold reserves to market quarterly and monthly, respectively. This means the gold reserves of the EUR and the CNY rise when gold rises. Both currencies strengthen when gold rises. Both currencies are aligned with the interests of EUR and CNY energy creditors, as opposed to the USD, which is aligned against US creditor interests.

Luke: Whoa…so this whole "leaving the USD" trend is not just driven by Russia and China and some other EMs?

Mr. X: Oh, no. The Europeans kicked it off back in 1999 with the EUR's formation when they surprisingly put 15 percent of Eurozone reserves into physical gold, marked to market quarterly. If the Europeans were so happy with USD hegemony, they never would've done that. They would've simply put those 15 percent of reserves into USTs and inextricably tied their fortunes to the USD forevermore, but they didn't.

It is not well understood among US investors that way back in 1999, the EU fired the first shot in what has come to be called a currency war with the rollout of the EUR. But that doesn't mean it isn't true.

Luke: So why didn't the Europeans tie themselves to the USD?

Mr. X: Because the people who run the EU are net creditors and net energy importers, which means it is a matter of national security to Germany and others to have and maintain cheap energy cost inputs of production.

This need is something probably deeply ingrained in the German psyche because lack of access to cheap oil is a key reason it lost World War II. Many World War II historians would tell you the Germans had better military equipment than most other combatants…but the United States and Russia had the cheap oil.

The EUR's architects must have understood that US entitlement obligations would eventually require massive USD printing, which (through the petrodollar link) would manifest as USD oil inflation—inflation that the EU, other net USD creditors, and net energy importers would have to pay…unless the EU came up with its own currency constructed in such a way as to preserve its energy creditors' purchasing power; those creditors would then have to be willing to sell oil cheaply in that currency.

Guess who else is a net exporter and net energy importer? China. And it is constructing the CNY in the same way as the EUR. Aligned with energy creditors.

Luke: Okay, so you're telling me that post-2008, once things were stabilized, the world essentially agreed to end the USD-centric petrodollar system in favor of a system where oil was priced in multiple currencies versus just USDs as had been the case since 1973, and, therefore, every nation either had to become oil independent or settle net oil imbalances with some sort of neutral settlement asset like physical gold instead of one nation's sovereign debt (USTs)?

Mr. X: I'm not telling you anything since I was not privy to any such discussions. I am merely describing what is happening as it is developing…. I am merely the little boy in this story noticing that the emperor has no clothes, if you will.

Luke: And so if this is the case, and if "somebody" continues not to allow USD gold prices to reflect the reality of physical demand seen since 2013, then the price of oil in USD must continue to fall…?

Mr. X: It sure seems that way, doesn't it?

Luke: So then how do we get out of this?

Mr. X: Do you know who William White is?

Luke: Yes. Former chief economist of the BIS. He famously warned of the 2008 crisis well ahead of time. A consummate insider, he spent thirty-nine years advising global central banks in a variety of capacities. Why?

Mr. X: He has recently begun making some interesting and vocal pronouncements.

[Mr. X pulled out a sheet of paper from his folder to read.]

Here's what he said on December 6, 2015 in an article titled "China begins G20 leadership with ideas to reduce USD's role":

> "We will need another global crisis, and one whose roots can be clearly identified in the shortcomings of the current non-system, for this to happen," said William White, an adviser to the Organization for Economic Cooperation and Development. The G-20's agenda can also become dominated by pressing issues of the moment.
>
> "I suspect that geopolitical issues will trump economic ones," White said.
>
> [http://www.bloomberg.com/news/articles/2015-12-06/china-starts-mapping-out-g-20-plan-after-year-of-market-turmoil]

Mr. X: More recently, William White warned of coming debt defaults and then used a most curious phrase: "Debt jubilees." [Mr. X turned the pages in his folder and found his source before continuing.] He was quoted in an article in the *Telegraph* on January 19, 2016, titled, "World Faces Wave of Epic Debt Defaults Fears Central Bank Veteran White."

> The global financial system has become dangerously unstable and faces an avalanche of bankruptcies that will test social and political stability, a leading monetary

theorist has warned. *"The situation is worse than it was in 2007. Our macroeconomic ammunition to fight downturns is essentially all used up,"* said William White, the Swiss-based chairman of the OECD's review committee and former chief economist of the BIS.

"It will become obvious in the next recession that many of these debts will never be serviced or repaid, and this will be uncomfortable for a lot of people who think they own assets that are worth something.... The only question is whether we are able to look reality in the eye and face what is coming in an orderly fashion, or whether it will be disorderly. *Debt jubilees have been going on for 5,000 years, as far back as the Sumerians."*

[http://www.telegraph.co.uk/finance/financetopics/davos/1 2108569/World-faces-wave-of-epic-debt-defaults-fears-central-bank-veteran.html. Emphasis mine.]

Luke: Fascinating comments coming from such a consummate insider—what do you make of them?

Mr. X: When I hear "debt jubilees," I think of unsecured lending. After all, debt that is collateralized doesn't need a jubilee; the lender simply repossesses the asset and takes any associated loss. So what is the biggest source of "unsecured lending" to be found in the world today?

Luke: Sovereign debt.

Mr. X: Correct! Sovereign debt. Full faith and credit and all that good stuff. Now because we have a system without a "neutral reserve asset," nations' unsecured sovereign debts are the assets of the rest of the world, no?

So we couldn't very easily simply just write off the world's sovereign debts in one big debt jubilee, now could we? Doing so would bankrupt the nations and wealthy elites holding those sovereign debts as their wealth! People would starve, and wars would be fought—not a good situation.

No, double-entry bookkeeping requires that any such "debt jubilee" (which I agree is necessary) must be accomplished not by writing down sovereign debt, but rather, by writing up some other asset that appears on every single Central Bank balance sheet, to keep the system whole.

Do you know of any neutral reserve asset that appears on every single global Central Bank balance sheet that can be inflated to infinity with no practical direct impact on the real economy because "it is not used for anything" and which global Central Banks have recently begun buying in record amounts for the first time in forty years? [Smiling.]

Luke: Gold…

Mr. X: Yes, that is the only asset I can think of too. And if the creditor nations are allowed to acquire gold at a low price ahead of any "debt jubilee" achieved by writing up gold against all currencies, should they care whether they hold USTs or gold as their reserve asset?

Luke: No, they wouldn't care. They only care about the ability of their FX reserves to buy them oil and other critical imported goods and services.

Mr. X: Correct. They only care about the ability of their FX reserves to buy them oil. So if we let oil exporters and creditors load up on gold and then massively devalue oil (and by extension, all currencies) against gold, do those oil exporters and creditors care?

Luke: No, they don't care because they have been made whole for past production surpluses through the write-up of gold. In other words, *a debt jubilee.*

Mr. X: Correct again, Luke. Exactly right. This is the real game that is afoot in my opinion. And it seems like we are "in the late innings," as I believe is said in America? As William White said, all that is needed is a crisis that indicts the current USD-centric system.

Luke: Yes...it's interesting then that all we hear on heavy repeat in Western financial media is how the strong USD and/or weak EM currencies are causing enormous problems, isn't it?

Mr. X: Indeed.

Luke: But this could go on for another year or more, couldn't it?

Mr. X: That depends on what happens to the price of oil after the CNY oil contract goes live, as well as what happens to the US fiscal situation.

Luke: Yes, but consensus is that the EMs will crash first, while the US will be the last man standing, just like in 1982 and 1998. Do you agree with that?

Mr. X: I think the world is a very different place today than what it was in 1998. EMs have $11T in FX reserves to burn that they didn't have then. The US Federal debt is over 100 percent of GDP, when in 1998 the US was running a surplus.

The US is now one of the world's three biggest oil producers and has a middle class that looks more like an EM than the US in 1998. So I think conventional wisdom may be in for a surprise this year, but let's assume it's not. Let me ask you a simple question:

Let's say oil stays around $40 and assume further that the US goes into a recession; who will buy the $1-2 trillion in UST issuance that is a virtual mathematical certainty in the case of a US recession in 2017E, especially since EMs will likely be selling another $750B to $1T in USTs in that case…not OPEC, not Russia, not China, not Europe…who? The Bank of Japan (BOJ) perhaps?

Luke: We've been wondering that same thing, but Wall Street isn't wondering it yet.

Mr. X: No, I agree Wall Street is not wondering that yet. But I think it may be interesting to watch how the USD trades once Wall Street starts wondering that same thing.

Luke: So if you had to guess the most likely path from here, how do you see all of this playing out?

Mr. X: If it's a crisis we need to drive changes that will be for the good of all in the world (except for Washington politicians and lobbyists), then maybe it's a crisis we will get.

Chapter 2

THE SECOND MEETING, BREAKFAST, JANUARY 2016

WHY NOW?

Luke: After dinner last night, I couldn't fall asleep for some time—our conversation kept rattling around in my head for half the night. It raised a number of questions I had to ask. So Mr. X, before we go any further, I'd like to back up a step and ask you: Why is this happening now?

Mr. X: What do you mean?

Luke: I mean you described some of the reasons why the world is "de-dollarizing" at an accelerating pace, so I guess I am looking for answers to the question "Why *now*?" What are the so-called "big gears" motivating the relevant parties to take the actions you described previously? Nobody wants a crisis per se, so what are the factors driving China, Russia, and others to push events toward the crisis you outlined?

Mr. X: Oh, I understand now. What is motivating the actors involved to do what they are doing? There are five historically-unique factors that no one alive has ever seen before: Demographics, Geology, Debt, Economic Reality, and the Repeated Weaponization of the Dollar.

Luke: Demographics, Geology, Debt, Economic Reality, and the Weaponization of the Dollar? Please elaborate.

Mr. X: Demographics is pretty straightforward—because of the US Baby Boomer generation, US entitlement programs that were long described as being problematic "someday" are now problematic "today." Those entitlement programs either already have or will soon move into what I would call "net disbursement mode."

Luke: Does "net disbursement mode" mean US entitlement programs are going free cash-flow negative for the first time ever?

Mr. X: Exactly…and estimates of the US' entitlement liabilities range from $100T to $200T+, depending on whom you ask. Against "just" $20T in US GDP and a relatively miniscule $3.3T in US Federal tax receipts, US entitlements going free cash-flow negative is a critically-important milestone.

Luke: Let me play devil's advocate here for a moment if I may: The US isn't the only nation with onerous entitlement obligations, right?

Mr. X: No, the US is not.

Luke: So then why are you picking on my beloved home country?

Mr. X: Because your country's currency has had a monopoly on the global pricing of oil and other commodities since 1973….

Luke: So what?

Mr. X: So when your nation prints the money to pay for those entitlements…and in my opinion it *will* print that money…your nation's actions will massively inflate the price of oil and other commodities for every other nation on the planet, and in particular, your biggest creditors. We saw this phenomenon play out on a much smaller scale in 2011.

Luke: What do you mean?

Mr. X: The US implemented Quantitative Easing (QE) in early 2009, and while the Fed and most US pundits claimed that QE did not spur inflation, many in China and the Middle East would beg to differ…remember the so-called "Arab Spring" in 2011? Food inflation played a contributing role, did it not?

Luke: Ah, I understand what you're saying. US QE did not create US inflation because it exported that inflation to its creditors through oil markets and US deficits.

Mr. X: Exactly! Now remember, that was *only* $3T or so in QE…and oil rose from $35 in 2008 to $120 in 2011. What would happen to the global price of oil and broader inflation rates in China, in the Middle East, in Russia, and at other US creditors if the US began printing large amounts of the $100T+ it owes its Baby Boomers?

Luke: We would cause borderline hyperinflation and likely social unrest in the Middle East and China.

Mr. X: Yes. Do you think the Chinese, with their reputation for planning far in advance, are going to sit around waiting for the US to begin hyperinflating the Chinese economy through the USD's link to oil and other commodities?

Luke: Probably not.

Mr. X: I would change that to definitely not. That is why the first factor I mentioned was "demographics." Virtually nobody sees it, but US entitlements are very similar in nature to the war reparations Germany owed to the Allies in the aftermath of World War I.

Luke: How so?

Mr. X: They are impossibly large relative to the size of US economic output, and they are inflation-adjusting—the US does not owe $100 trillion in entitlements in "USDs"; it owes them in "medical goods and services," so as the US prints money to pay for those "medical goods and services," the law of supply and demand means that the price of those "medical goods and services" should rise. This means that unless the US government wants to steal real purchasing power from its healthcare sector (pay US doctors and other service providers less than rate of inflation), these entitlement obligations will only grow bigger. As it stands today, the cost of servicing those entitlements has already long been rising (and likely will continue to rise) well in excess of US inflation metrics.

Luke: Whoa…I never thought of it like that. It does not paint a pretty picture for the USD, does it?

Mr. X: No, it does not. And that is why China, Russia, and other US creditors are so motivated by the first factor I mentioned: demographics.

Luke: How about the second factor you mentioned: geology?

Mr. X: This one is pretty straightforward. USD cost curves of the world's marginal oil supplies have shifted markedly higher over the past decade.

Luke: Why is that so important?

Mr. X: Let's pretend you're China with $3T in FX reserves, yielding right around 0 percent. You know your oil consumption needs are going to continue rising at a rapid clip well into the future, and that your own domestic oil production has begun falling. If your $3T "savings account" (those FX reserves) is yielding 0 percent and the cost of finding new oil is rising sharply in USD terms globally, what is happening to the real value of your FX reserves "savings account"?

Luke: It's falling sharply.

Mr. X: It's falling sharply. Exactly. This is critical to understand—it's a very American thing to think of global FX reserves balances in USD terms, but you would be better-served to think of them in oil terms, because that is how much of the world thinks of them, and it is certainly how China thinks of them.

China is not stupid. It does not want to save its surpluses in a currency that pays it no yield and which is virtually guaranteed to lose purchasing power versus critical economic inputs (oil, food, and other commodities) without which its people will suffer high rates of inflation, eventually causing domestic Chinese social instability that the Chinese Communist Party is determined to avoid at all costs.

Luke: Well, when you put it that way, it makes perfect sense...but it begs another question: If, between the US demographic issues and global geology issues you raised, China knows USDs will not be a good store of value for future oil imports, what can China do?

Mr. X: A terrific question—perhaps *the* most important question. China has two choices—it can either find a lot more oil, or it can pay for oil in a better currency than the USD.

Luke: A better currency than the USD? Most on Wall Street would tell you there *is* no such thing!

Mr. X: Most on Wall Street also told me that US home prices could never fall nationally, didn't they?

Luke: Ouch...and yes, they did. So what is the better currency China could pay in?

Mr. X: Well, for China, the best currency to pay for oil imports would be the currency it could print, no?

Luke: Well, sure! But what oil importer would be willing to take the CNY over the USD?

Mr. X: Again, that is the crux of the issue. On the merits of each, I doubt any oil exporter would take CNY over the USD...but that is where gold comes into play.

Luke: Come again?

Mr. X: Oh, I agree, few if any oil exporters would trust the CNY over the USD...but let me tell you in no uncertain terms: *Every* oil exporter would take real, physical gold for its oil over the USD.

By extension, any such oil exporters would be willing to take CNY if the Chinese were to reopen the gold window that President Nixon closed so many years ago, using the CNY and a variety of CNY-denominated gold contracts all over the world.

Luke: Which is exactly what China has been doing....

Mr. X: Which is exactly what China has been doing. Most on Wall Street don't understand this.... They look at what China has been doing with gold and laugh because they are just as sure that gold isn't used for anything as they once were that US home prices could never fall nationally.

Well, I think China may get the last laugh on this matter. Wall Street doesn't understand that what China is doing with gold is not about gold; it's about oil...and more specifically, the ability to print CNY for oil. That is the Holy Grail because it gives China its economic and monetary independence from the USD. China is playing chess while most of Wall Street and Washington are playing tic-tac-toe...or perhaps more apropos, China is playing "Go."

Luke: Wow...so is China effectively making plans to back the CNY with gold?

Mr. X: No, no, no...as we discussed earlier, it's far more subtle than that. It is not backing the CNY with gold; it is effectively reopening the Bretton Woods gold window that the US closed in 1971, except China is reopening the gold window through CNYs instead of USDs.

Luke: Okay, but isn't that a gold standard?

Mr. X: It would be, but for one key difference: The Chinese are not making the same mistakes the US did with Bretton Woods.... It is not fixing the CNY price of gold; it is allowing gold to float. By the way, this is similar to the way the EUR treats gold with its quarterly marking to market of gold reserves.

Additionally, China is also avoiding another US Bretton Woods mistake vis-à-vis gold by not allowing gold stored in Mainland China to leave Mainland China.

Luke: But if the price of gold will float in CNY (and EUR), doesn't this encourage deflation in gold terms in those currencies?

Mr. X: That's what some neoliberal economists might tell you, but they are only looking at it with a very narrow lens. But through my lens, I view what China is doing quite differently....

Luke: How would you look at it?

Mr. X: Through my lens, what China is doing encourages oil exporters to sell oil to China in CNY because they understand that by allowing gold to float in CNY terms, China is communicating to oil exporters that oil exporters' purchasing power will be maintained in those currencies through the floating gold link.

And by the way, this is *exactly* the same way gold is treated by the Eurozone and the EUR....

Luke: What an elegant idea—a mutually-agreeable, win/win currency system....

Mr. X: As opposed to the USD, which as we have long seen, must steal purchasing power from its creditors just to maintain the solvency of the US government.

Luke: Steal purchasing power from creditors via QE?

Mr. X: Via deficit spending, and then once the US financial system imploded, via QE...which is probably a good segue to the next reason all of this is happening now.

Luke: But first, why would the US care if China or any other nation is pricing and settling oil and other commodity trade in CNY or EUR or whatever?

Mr. X: Because if China can effectively print CNY for oil, then it can reduce its FX reserves. China will then become just the second nation in the world in the past seventy years to be able to print currency for oil. The practical implications of this can be seen in a chart I have to share with you.

[Mr. X turned a page in his folder and pulled out the following chart.]

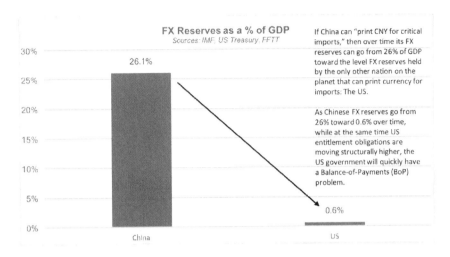

FX Reserves as a % of GDP
Sources: IMF, US Treasury, FFTT

If China can "print CNY for critical imports," then over time its FX reserves can go from 26% of GDP toward the level FX reserves held by the only other nation on the planet that can print currency for imports: The US.

As Chinese FX reserves go from 26% toward 0.6% over time, while at the same time US entitlement obligations are moving structurally higher, the US government will quickly have a Balance-of-Payments (BoP) problem.

As noted in the chart, if China can effectively print CNY for oil like the US, then over time, China's FX reserve needs will become like those of the United States, falling from 26 percent of GDP to the United States' 0.6 percent of GDP. Of course, such a move will not happen overnight, but it *will* immediately reduce China's appetite for USTs...whose balances have been rising at $1.2T per year for the past nine years....

[As he spoke, Mr. X showed me two more charts.]

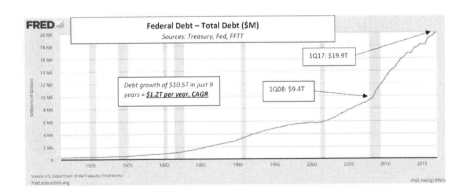

...as US Federal spending on Healthcare, Entitlements, and Defense have exploded higher due to US demographics and expensive perpetual wars on terror:

Mr. X: These charts show why there will be an issue for the United States Federal deficit if multi-currency oil pricing takes hold: If other nations can print their own currency for oil, those nations do *not* need nearly as many USDs and, therefore, do *not* need to fund US deficits (driven mainly by US Entitlements and Defense spending.)

Luke: Let's see; the third reason you mentioned was...debt. What do you mean by that?

Mr. X: Simple—global debt levels have reached all-time record highs and interest rates have hit 5,000 year lows. If your nation earns its income by exporting a finite product (oil and other commodities or hard goods), you would have to be stupid to stockpile your national surpluses in the sovereign debts of nations with record high levels of debt and record low levels of interest rates.

Luke: Why do you say "you would have to be stupid"?

Mr. X: Because throughout history, all sovereigns eventually default once debts get too high. Always. They may nominally default or they may default in real terms (i.e., via inflation), but they always default. There is no sovereign that has never defaulted.

Luke: People tell me all the time that the United States has never defaulted!

Mr. X: That's not true. The United States has defaulted twice in the past eighty-five years alone—once on gold contract clauses in 1933, when FDR suspended the gold standard and then devalued the USD versus gold by 65 percent, and then again in 1971, when Richard Nixon closed the gold window to US foreign creditors.

Luke: Most Americans would tell you those were not defaults.

Mr. X: If the Americans who say that actually believe it, then they are welcome to work in my home for one million dollars per year for the next ten years, with the entire sum to be paid in arrears at the end of ten years.

Luke: Sounds like a great deal…I might be interested. What's the catch?

Mr. X: The "catch" is that at the end of ten years, I will pay them in Zimbabwe rather than US dollars.

Luke: Never mind. I'm no longer interested in working in your house. And let me guess—that is akin to what FDR and Nixon did to US foreign creditors.

Mr. X: Yes, that is akin to what FDR and Nixon did to US foreign creditors; not to this extreme, of course, but it was directionally the same thing…switching terms from a superior to an inferior currency after the fact.

Luke: Which is why China, Russia, and others want to get away from USDs.

Mr. X: Luke, your generation is too young to remember that sovereigns always end up defaulting. It has never not happened. It simply happens so rarely that by the time it happens again, everyone who was investing the last time it happened is already dead. It is an easily-studied long cycle phenomenon—Ken Rogoff and Carmen Reinhart wrote about it in a paradoxically-named paper and book of the same name: *It's Different This Time*. But most investors are too busy or too hubristic to read history books....

Luke: When was the last time this happened globally?

Mr. X: In the 1930s.

Luke: And were there lots of defaults?

Mr. X: Allow me to read you a couple of lines from Liaquat Ahamed's excellent *Lords of Finance*: *The Bankers Who Broke the World*, a biopic of the world's four major Central Bankers the last time the world was in a global sovereign debt crisis.

[Mr. X turned a page in his folder and found the passage.]

> Pg 143: "France eventually settled its war debts to the US for $0.40 on the dollar; Italy for $0.26."

> Pg 467: "The only country that eventually paid the Americans in full on their war debts was Finland."

Luke: Good God...nobody on Wall Street realizes this is coming.

Mr. X: No, they don't, but judging by their actions, global Central Banks do.

Luke: What do you mean?

Mr. X: Since the second quarter of 2013 up until now in early 2016, global Central Banks have bought far more gold than USTs…did you know that?

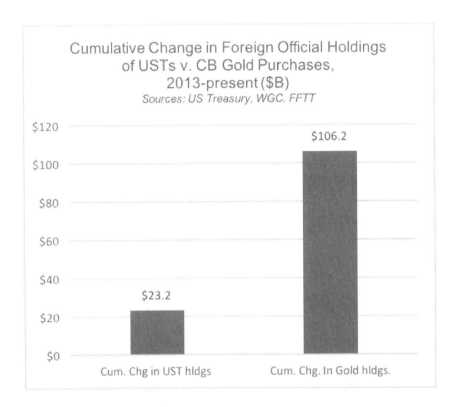

Luke: Wow. Why do you think Wall Street just ignores this?

Mr. X: Because Wall Street is generally a young man's game, and as I said before, young men generally don't learn anything from history until it happens to them. Many of the people ignoring Central Bank gold purchases and saying gold isn't used for anything are the same types of people (and in some cases the exact same people) who said, "US home prices could never fall nationally."

They simply do not have the historical perspective to consider what could happen because it has not happened in their lifetimes, and therefore, they suffer from recency bias. It's not their fault though—it's just human nature. It's this same recency bias that causes investors to ignore the next reason all this is happening as well.

Luke: That must be "Economic Reality"? What do you mean by that?

Mr. X: Yes. China is now the world's biggest oil importer, and EMs are the majority share of global GDP for the first time in more than 300 years. When the US overtook England as the world's biggest energy importer and country, it decided it would transact in USDs. So why is it that Western investors are so blind to the inevitability that China and EMs will cut out the USD now that they are in the position the US once was and the US is in the position the UK once was?

Luke: I don't know—recency bias? Hubris?

Mr. X: I think Western investors see it happening, but they just think these trends move so slowly that it won't matter for a long time, not any time soon. But in my opinion, that is the chief fault in their logic. That's probably also why they completely ignore any potential blowback that might occur from the last reason, the repeated weaponization of the USD.

Luke: What do you mean?

Mr. X: Oh, I agree with investors that these trends move very slowly, that they take a long time to play out…but there comes a time when they go from impossible to inevitable without ever stopping at improbable, and they often do so extraordinarily rapidly.

Luke: Reminds me of Bear Stearns or Lehman Brothers—seemed obvious in hindsight, and things moved slowly, and then they moved very rapidly.

Mr. X: Yes…and that is my point. We are not months into this trend, Luke. China was admitted to the WTO fifteen years ago. The Euro began trading seventeen years ago. The US financial system was shown to be made of "balsa wood and baby tears" eight years ago. China and Iran began transacting oil in CNY four years ago. Global FX reserves peaked and began falling eighteen ago. China and Russia began transacting oil in non-USD nearly two years ago.

Many of these trends are very mature, yet virtually no Western investors are talking about them…and they likely won't until it becomes very obvious. But markets are already beginning to play by the new rules, which confuses many investors. One of my favorite market quotes comes from Bob Farrell, the long-time Merrill Lynch strategist:

> Change of a long term or secular nature is usually gradual enough that it is obscured by the noise caused by short-term volatility. By the time secular trends are even acknowledged by the majority, they are generally obvious and mature.
>
> In the early stages of a new secular paradigm, most are conditioned to hear only the short-term noise they have been conditioned to respond to by the prior existing secular condition. Moreover, in a shift of secular or long-term

significance, the markets will be adapting to a new set of rules, while most market participants will still be playing by the old rules.

Luke: So then, what are the new rules the market is playing by?

Mr. X: They aren't really new rules…the rules themselves are centuries old. The rules are only "new" to those who don't pay attention to the history books! The "new" old rules are straightforward, related, and all driven by China's desire to create an escape valve to get away from the aforementioned five factors we discussed:

1. US deficits have begun to matter again for the first time in seventy years.

2. China is "reopening the Bretton Woods gold window at a floating price through CNY" as a means to an end: To gain the ability to print CNY for oil and other critical commodities.

Luke: "New Old Rules"…I like that description. I'm definitely going to keep a close eye on those two new "old" rules.

Mr. X: Good. If you keep a close eye on them, you will be part of a very small club. Most of Wall Street seems to be completely ignoring these "new old rules." I suspect by the time this cycle is over, they may come to regret that oversight.

Luke: Thanks again for your time, Mr. X.

Mr. X: Until next time, my friend.

Chapter 3

THE THIRD CONVERSATION, DINNER, FEBRUARY 2017

PERHAPS THE CRISIS SO MANY HAVE BEEN LOOKING FOR IN THE MARKETS HAS BEGUN ARRIVING AT THE BALLOT BOX!

Luke: Mr. X, the last time we sat down to dinner, you said we'd need a crisis to drive change…but there have been no crises in the markets, so do you think the systemic changes you detailed then have stopped or even reversed?

Mr. X: No, because like you are assuming now, I once assumed the needed crisis would take place in financial markets. But if we take a broader view, or just ask a member of the global political class, it seems as if populism represents a dire crisis indeed; does it not? Perhaps the crisis has begun arriving at the ballot box! Let me read you a passage from an article in the *New York Times* on November 9, 2016 following Donald Trump's election as President of the United States.

[Mr. X turned a page in his folder and then read the following passage.]

Donald Trump Is Elected President in Stunning Repudiation of the Establishment – *NYT*, 11/9/16

Donald John Trump was elected the 45th president of the United States on Tuesday in a stunning culmination of an explosive, populist and polarizing campaign that took relentless aim at the institutions and long-held ideals of American democracy.

The surprise outcome, defying late polls that showed Hillary Clinton with a modest but persistent edge, threatened convulsions throughout the country and the world, where skeptics had watched with alarm as Mr. Trump's unvarnished overtures to disillusioned voters took hold.

The triumph for Mr. Trump, 70, a real estate developer-turned-reality television star with no government experience, was a powerful rejection of the establishment forces that had assembled against him, from the world of business to government, and the consensus they had forged on everything from trade to immigration.

[https://www.nytimes.com/2016/11/09/us/politics/hillary-clinton-donald-trump-president.html?_r=0]

Luke: What do you make of the election of Donald Trump?

Mr. X: What was it I said to you earlier? "If it is a crisis we need to drive changes that will be for the good of all in the world (except for Washington politicians and lobbyists), then it is a crisis we will get"?

Well, I and many others thought that such a crisis was likely to transpire in global markets, but to my eyes, it appears as if it may instead have arrived in the form of a political crisis! I must say, I think Trump's victory may represent an accelerant of some of the major global changes already underway that we discussed previously.

Luke: Besides the obvious, are you seeing anything else that makes you think that?

Mr. X: Yes. I have been fascinated to watch the reaction of some of the most politically-connected neoliberal economists in the US—Paul Krugman, Larry Summers, Justin Wolfers, etc. Their criticisms of Trump's economic plans seem almost irrationally angry. I've brought you a list of some of those criticisms that you can read on your own.

[Mr. X passed to me a sheet of paper with the following notations.]

Krugman: "Deficits good" on 10/22/16, "Deficits bad" on 1/9/17—why the change in just a three-month period?

http://krugman.blogs.nytimes.com/2016/10/22/debt-diversion-distraction/

https://www.nytimes.com/2017/01/09/opinion/deficits-matter-again.html?_r=0

Summers: Trump economic plan "voodoo", "economic creationism" – 1/3/17
http://money.cnn.com/2017/01/04/news/economy/larry-summers-navarro-ross-voodoo/

Wolfers: Trump favors small business v. academic economists – 1/11/17

https://www.nytimes.com/2017/01/11/upshot/why-most-economists-are-so-worried-about-trump.html

Luke: Why do you think those aforementioned economists are seemingly so "irrationally angry," as you put it?

Mr. X: As someone once said, "Follow the money."

Luke: What do you mean?

Mr. X: What has the United States' largest export been for the last twenty years or so?

Luke: I don't know—Aerospace/Defense, or maybe technology?

Mr. X: No, not even close. The United States' largest export for the last twenty years or so has easily been USDs &/or USTs.

[Mr. X now turned another page in his folder and handed me another chart.]

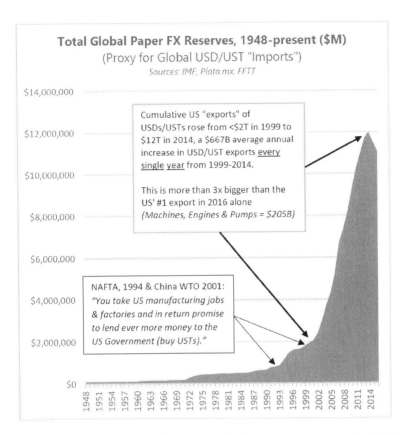

Total Global Paper FX Reserves, 1948-present ($M)
(Proxy for Global USD/UST "Imports")
Sources: IMF, Plata.nx, FFTT

Cumulative US "exports" of USDs/USTs rose from <$2T in 1999 to $12T in 2014, a $667B average annual increase in USD/UST exports every single year from 1999-2014.

This is more than 3x bigger than the US' #1 export in 2016 alone (Machines, Engines & Pumps = $205B)

NAFTA, 1994 & China WTO 2001: "You take US manufacturing jobs & factories and in return promise to lend ever more money to the US Government (buy USTs)."

While exact data is hard to come by, by one measure, the US has exported between $5T and $10T in USDs/USTs in just the past fifteen years, depending on what we assume the USD's share of global FX reserves to be.

Now, Luke, I am sure if anyone can do so, you can tell me what all those USD and UST exports paid for, right?

Luke: US Federal Entitlements and Defense spending?

Mr. X: Exactly…Entitlements and Defense.

[Mr. X turned to another chart showing the Eleven Largest Outlays with the Entitlements and Defense on the bottom of the chart.]

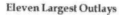

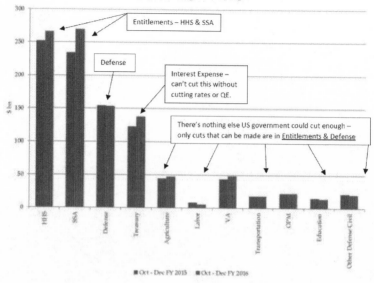

Source: United States Department of the Treasury

Luke: Okay, so if the US' biggest exports over the past 15-20 years have been USDs/USTs by far, then wouldn't it stand to reason that the US regions that produce and export USDs and USTs would benefit most from this status quo?

Mr. X: Yes…so tell me, what region of the US produces and exports USTs?

Luke: Washington, DC?

Mr. X: You got it. Most people don't think of it that way, but the data show it to be true, whether you consider the number of jobs in the US in manufacturing versus government… [Here Mr. X showed me a chart comparing US employees in manufacturing versus government.]

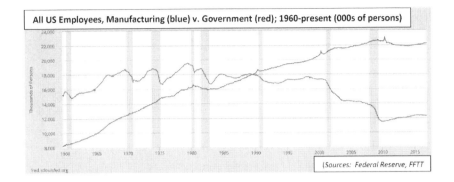

All US Employees, Manufacturing (blue) v. Government (red); 1960-present (000s of persons)

(Sources: Federal Reserve, FFTT)

...or in the pay of those jobs—no less than the *Washington Post* noted in 2012 that seven of the US' ten most affluent counties are in the Washington, DC region—that is no coincidence!

Luke: With all due respect, Mr. X, wouldn't the neoliberal economists we highlighted earlier in this chapter tell us that those manufacturing jobs were all going to go away as a result of automation? And so, Keynesian theory tells us the US government must step up to fill the gap. And that's what it did—by creating higher-paying US government jobs no less?

Mr. X: They would tell us that, and they often do tell us that. There are just two problems with that as I see it.

The first problem is that the data tells us the neoliberal "automation took manufacturing jobs" narrative is wrong—US manufacturing jobs fell by 5.5m from 2002 to 2009 shortly after China was granted "Most Favored Nation" trading status under the WTO in 2001. I struggle to think of an automation technology advancement that would explain this big a drop occurring in so short a time.

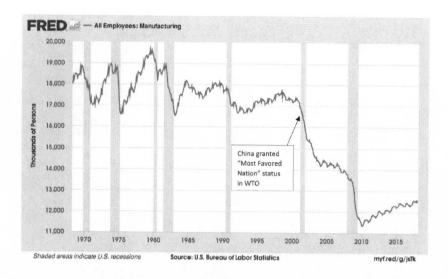

FRED — All Employees: Manufacturing

Shaded areas indicate U.S. recessions   Source: U.S. Bureau of Labor Statistics   myf.red/g/jsTk

The second problem is the one we are now facing—if the deal was "You take our manufacturing jobs and facilities and, in return, you buy our USTs to fund US government deficits," then what happens when US foreign official creditors like China decide to stop buying USTs to fund US Federal deficits? This question is relevant because in November 2013, the People's Bank of China (PBOC) formally announced, and I quote, "It is no longer in China's favor to boost record FX reserves." In other words, in late 2013, China announced it was no longer in China's favor to stockpile USTs ad infinitum.

Luke: We have written numerous times that the answer to your question "What happens when US foreign official creditors stop funding the US?" is "Longstanding US Balance-of-Payments (BoP) imbalances finally begin to manifest themselves in LIBOR & UST yields and elsewhere," no?

Mr. X: Exactly. Look, I said "Follow the money" because money is power. As long as USDs/USTs are the United States' biggest exports, the US government, and in particular Washington, is concentrating global power on a relative basis, even if that leads to what the data showed earlier, which is a hollowing out of the US manufacturing sector and middle classes.

This is why I have been so fascinated by the vitriolic reactions of these establishment economists—they are supporters of the status quo in a big, big way. That they are reacting the way they are to Trump suggests to me that Trump represents a potential significant power shift away from the Washington-centric currency system they have grown up under and indeed created.

Luke: Let's take a bit of a step back here: Why do you think Trump won?

Mr. X: If you read economic history, you learn there are long cycles to everything. In my opinion, Trump won because US elites and especially US economic elites overreached, as history tells us they always do.

Luke: I agree with you, but please elaborate on how you think they overreached this time.

Mr. X: Let's look at some maps. [He pulled out two maps of the United States.] Over the last twenty-five years, Washington leaders have followed the policies espoused by many of these same neoliberal economists, and as we showed before, Washington (and the US coasts) prospered while over the past fifteen years "flyover country" has seen an estimated 100,000-500,000 excess deaths [He pulled out two articles he handed to me, listed below] from what is at its core "economic hopelessness" (suicides, drug overdoses, alcoholism), etc.

Perhaps I am oversimplifying, but once your economic policies begin driving your nation's life expectancy down via an estimated 100,000-500,000 premature deaths, it may be time to rethink your positions, no?

US Life expectancy falls 1ˢᵗ time in 23 years with rises in 8 of 10 leading causes of death – 12/18/16

http://www.telegraph.co.uk/news/2016/12/08/us-life-expectancy-falls-first-time-23-years-rises-8-10-leading/

Death rates rising for middle aged white Americans – 11/3/15

http://www.nytimes.com/2015/11/03/health/death-rates-rising-for-middle-aged-white-americans-study-finds.html

Luke: So you think Trump's victory was in a way a repudiation of academic economists' neoliberal policies implemented by Washington over the past 20-30 years?

Mr. X: Yes, I do. To my eyes, this is simple Maslow's Hierarchy of Needs-type stuff. If you can't afford to feed your family, issues that economic elites typically spend time at Davos talking about cease to matter to the average person. At its core, Trump's economic message was "I'll change things so you can afford to feed your family again." It's how and why he flipped Ohio, Michigan, Pennsylvania, and Wisconsin to his side, which is how he won the election.

Luke: All else equal, what you say was Trump's core economic message seems like a net positive for the US, so why are so many prominent academic economists so upset?

Mr. X: Again, this is my opinion, but I think it is because they fear that the changes Trump was advertising in his campaign and now appears to be preparing for via his cabinet appointments may change the global money system away from the USD-centric status quo that those economists espoused.

Luke: How and why will Trump do that?

Mr. X: I thought Hugo Salinas-Price made an excellent point in this article from January 10, 2017 that answers your question. [Mr. X read to me the following piece]:

Trump's Ignorance

If Mr. Trump should attempt to eliminate or reduce the US trade deficit and protect and encourage US reindustrialization by means of tariffs on imports, what he would achieve would be to choke the economies of the rest of the world with a scarcity of dollars obtained—how else?—by exports to the US.

Choking on dollar scarcity, because exports to the US decline or are eliminated, the world will not remain in paralysis. Another alternative to the dollar as the world's currency will be sought, simply because finding an alternative becomes a matter of life or death.

Mr. Trump does not know it, but applying a policy of protectionism for American industry through tariffs on imports means the death of the world's monetary system based on the dollar.

[http://www.plata.com.mx/mplata/articulos/articlesFilt.asp?fiidarticulo=303. Emphasis is Mr. Salinas-Price's.]

Luke: But in the article, Salinas-Price says Trump doesn't know what he's doing.

Mr. X: Yes, and perhaps Salinas-Price is right, but I think Trump knows exactly what he's doing. I mean, look at who he has appointed to his cabinet. The new US National Economic Director is the former COO of Goldman Sachs. In my opinion, it stretches credulity to think Gary Cohn doesn't know what he's doing on these topics.

Furthermore, it was pointed out to me recently that at least one Wall Street firm recently noted that Trump's policy goals to-date have been vague with one exception—his goals on trade and FX. There it was noted by Nomura: "One of the most remarkable aspects of [Trump's] plan is the level of detail and the citation of US Acts of law that could be invoked. In no other areas of policy has he done this." [Source: Bilal Hafeez, Nomura Securities (h/t DC.)]

Are we to believe that Trump and his team have looked in detail into US Acts of law that could be invoked to achieve their stated goals in trade (and by extension FX markets)? Trump's advisor's comments have been clear, yet are we to believe Trump's team doesn't know what it is doing vis-à-vis Salinas-Price's point? I don't know about you, but that strikes me as unlikely.

Luke: I agree.

Mr. X: Furthermore, judging by the reactions of some of the most politically well-connected US academic neoliberal economists, it appears they also believe Trump knows exactly what he and his cabinet are doing. Let me just quote from one. This is Paul Krugman to Bernard Lietaer. It's taken from a video titled "Never touch the money system...NEVER touch the money system!"

Now, Paul Krugman told me personally, that it was totally crazy to talk about the money issue. We were both from MIT, we graduated from the same school, we had the same professors, right? Here's what he told me:

Didn't they tell you?! Never touch the money system! NEVER touch the money system! You can touch everything else…never touch the money system…You will not be invited to the right places, and you can kiss goodbye the Nobel and anything else that is worthwhile getting. You're killing yourself academically if you touch the money system.

[https://www.youtube.com/watch?v=Q6nL9elK0E Y]

There are numerous others, including the ones listed earlier.

Mr. X: In my opinion, it is quite possible that these economists are losing their minds about Trump because they are beginning to fear, based on Trump's comments, that he is going to "change the money system," or as the *Wall Street Journal* noted per this quote:

This year, academic [economists] are out in the cold. During the election, *The Wall Street Journal* contacted every former member of the CEA, including those going back to President Richard Nixon. None had been tapped as an adviser to Mr. Trump's campaign, nor did any publicly endorse him.

The president-elect is "not particularly interested in hearing from the academic economist club," Mr. Davis said.

[Top economists grapple with public disdain for initiatives they championed – 1/8/17

http://www.wsj.com/articles/top-economists-grapple-with-public-disdain-for-initiatives-they-championed-1483916701]

Mr. X: Larry Summers' comments in particular are fascinating because, on one hand, he appears to have just woken up to the reality that the policies he and other neoliberal academic economists have espoused over the past 15-20 years have created enormous economic hardship in "flyover country." Here are some of his tweets after having read the book *Hillbilly Elegy: A Memoir of a Family and Culture in Crisis* by J. D. Vance that, in essence, detailed the lives of poor white people in the Midwest whom Trump mobilized to win the White House:

> I learned much from @HillbillyElegy that I should have known but really didn't. – Larry Summers, 2 January 2017, via Twitter

> Not much is more important than figuring out what to do about the issues that @HillbillyElegy so powerfully points up. – Larry Summers, 2 January 2017, via Twitter

> Reading about @HillbillyElegy is not [the] same as reading it. Anyone wanting to understand Trump's rise or American inequality should read it. – Larry Summers, 2 January 2017, via Twitter

> @HillbillyElegy demonstrates the power of economic forces and the limits of economic & statistical analysis. Every policy oriented economist should read @HillbillyElegy – Larry Summers, 2 January 2017, via Twitter

Mr. X: However, after appearing to understand that something has gone very wrong in "flyover country," in basically the very next breath, Summers goes right back to bashing Trump's economic plan as "economic voodoo or creationism," despite the likelihood that Trump's economic plan (all else equal) would go a long way in helping the very people Summers claims to want to help in his Tweetstorm of January 2, 2017.

Now, some might see Trump's unwillingness to consult with mainstream neoliberal academic economists as just another sign of Trump's hubris. However, students of history would do well to notice that it was only when FDR, Winston Churchill, and other political leaders of the day *stopped* listening to the orthodox economists of the day and began acting on their own to devalue their currencies that the worst economic aspects of the last global sovereign debt crisis (in the 1930s) began to recede.

Luke: Okay, to play devil's advocate, are there any other signs you're watching that might signal that Trump is getting ready to "change the money system"?

Mr. X: Absolutely, and they're hiding in plain sight.

Luke: What do you mean?

Mr. X: Well, we already established that the biggest beneficiary of the status quo "money system" has been Washington, DC, no? Knowing this, let me ask you: In your life, do you ever recall a president-elect being faced with the degree of pushback from various parts of the Washington establishment as Trump was?

Luke: No, I do not, but what informational value are you taking from this?

Mr. X: Remember, money is power. The previous charts I showed you reflect that Washington has benefited to the detriment of the rest of the United States by virtue of the "money system" some of these academic economists espoused over the past 20-30 years and continue to vehemently defend…and that Trump appears to want to change that money system to help "flyover country," "Hillary's deplorables," whatever you want to call it.

That's my read on it. I think Trump wants to change the money system from one that has benefitted Washington DC to the detriment of flyover country, to one that will begin to do the opposite (at least initially.) It appears I may not be the only one thinking in these terms. Here's a list of articles in agreement with me:

> **Nikkei: "Trump's tolerance of strong USD unlikely to last" – 12/29/16**
>
> http://asia.nikkei.com/Markets/Currencies/Trump-s-tolerance-of-strong-dollar-unlikely-to-last
>
> **Bundesbank brings home "significantly more gold in 2016 again than initially planned" – Weidmann, 12/23/16**
>
> http://www.reuters.com/article/germany-bundesbank-gold-idUSL5N1EI4IY
>
> **Putin says Trump is a smart man, will adapt as unipolar world model fails, balance restored – 12/4/16**
>
> http://www.zerohedge.com/news/2016-12-04/putin-says-trump-smart-man-will-adapt-responsibilities-unipolar-world-model-fails

Luke: But it appears as though not all of what you'd call the Washington establishment or status quo is against him…not all of Wall Street is against him, judging by his cabinet selections…. Why not?

Mr. X: I suspect it's because those people are both students of history and understand that the current system has outlived its usefulness to the United States, including to Washington, DC, even if most of Washington doesn't understand that yet.

Luke: What do you mean?

Mr. X: History is clear on this count—finance follows production/manufacturing, not the other way around. The United States became the biggest producer/manufacturer the world had ever seen to that point by running basically the same playbook that China has used since 1994. It was only after the United States became a big producer that it became a financial center as it used its productive output as leverage to drive favorable terms of finance for US industry and the US government.

Luke: Okay, go on...

Mr. X: Fast forward to today and China is now "factory to the world," and per history, China wants to leverage its productive output to gain control of the financial terms of trade for China.

[Mr. X passed a list of the following arguments to me to support his argument.]

> **"More than 25% of China's trade is now settled in CNY" – HSBC, 12/30/16**
>
> www.rmb.hsbc.com/~/media/files/renminbi-internationalisation-survey-2016-results.pdf
>
> **USD share of global currency reserves falls for 3rd straight quarter in 3Q16 – 1/2/17**
>
> http://mobile.reuters.com/article/idUSKBN14J1BV?il=0

China reduces USD's weighting in currency basket – 12/29/16

https://www.bloomberg.com/news/articles/2016-12-29/china-reduces-dollar-weighting-in-currency-basket-adds-11-more

China continues to unload US debt "for yuan's SDR entry" after which "more countries and regions will accept it" – *China People's Daily*, 9/19/16

http://en.people.cn/business/n3/2016/0919/c90778-9116583.html#.V9-2SIwLG64.twitter

Mr. X: If China is now factory to the world, it can increasingly set the terms of trade most favorable to it and cut out the USD, and by extension, simultaneously cease funding Washington deficits (and China's military encirclement by Washington) as well as gain share of global financial transactions from New York City over time. You can see this happening if you are looking for the critical tipping points as they rush by:

[Mr. X pointed at a sheet of paper with the following articles listed on it.

Emerging Markets to produce majority of global goods & services for 1st time in over 200 years – *Financial Times*, 6/3/13

India surpasses UK in terms of GDP for the 1st time in 150 years – 12/21/16

http://indianexpress.com/article/business/economy/india-surpasses-uk-in-terms-of-gdp-for-the-first-time-in-150-years-what-it-means-4438488/

Mr. X: I suspect that forward thinkers in the United States and in Trump's cabinet specifically understand the implications of the above.

Luke: Which is what?

Mr. X: With each passing day, the rest of the world needs the USD less and less. The reality is the only thing the rest of the world currently needs the USD for is to service large amounts of USD-denominated debt…. Everything else it needs it can increasingly get with CNY, JPY, EUR, or even RUB (in the case of energy). As Hugo Salinas-Price noted, if the US keeps using the USD to choke off the world, the world will just ditch the USD. An alternative system seems nearly ready to go.

Luke: So what is the solution you think "forward thinkers" in Trump's cabinet realize and are working on?

Mr. X: The US must begin to bring production assets back to US shores if New York City is to be able to compete globally with Asia in the long-term as a financial center. If China and Asia produce everything the world needs and then demand to be paid in CNY instead of USD (which is exactly what they are already into the middle innings of doing), both Washington, and arguably more importantly, New York City may find themselves on the outside of a New World Order, looking in.

Luke: Do you really think there are people in the US who understand this?

Mr. X: I suspect they are relatively few at this point, but they are there…. There are many brilliant people in your country!

Luke: You also noted that the current "money system" has outlived its usefulness to the United States. What did you mean by that?

Mr. X: Remember, as Hugo Salinas-Price noted, the Bretton Woods/USD reserve agreement was effectively a deal with the devil. In the near-term and medium-term, the US effectively swapped jobs and productive capacity for a debt-fueled Federal government- and consumer-spending binge, understanding that the long-term outcome would be US bankruptcy. This situation was laid out in the 1960s by Robert Triffin.

Well, as has a way of happening, the long term has now arrived and the devil wants his due. For Wall Street and the US consumer, the devil's due began in 2008. For Washington and other Western political centers, it began in the summer of 2016 with Brexit and continued last fall with Trump.

Luke: How do you think international elites feel about it?

Mr. X: I think they have long known the USD-centric system has been increasingly unstable and they have been looking for a way or reason to change the system. Remember what William White said a year ago:

> The global financial system has become dangerously unstable and faces an avalanche of bankruptcies that will test social and political stability, a leading monetary theorist has warned. *"The situation is worse than it was in 2007. Our macroeconomic ammunition to fight downturns is essentially all used up,"* said William White, the Swiss-based chairman of the OECD's review committee and former chief economist of the BIS.

"It will become obvious in the next recession that many of these debts will never be serviced or repaid, and this will be uncomfortable for a lot of people who think they own assets that are worth something"…. The only question is whether we are able to look reality in the eye and face what is coming in an orderly fashion, or whether it will be disorderly. *Debt jubilees have been going on for 5,000 years, as far back as the Sumerians."*

[World faces wave of epic debt defaults fears Central Bank veteran White – 1/19/16

http://www.telegraph.co.uk/finance/financetopics/davos/12108569/World-faces-wave-of-epic-debt-defaults-fears-central-bank-veteran.html]

Luke: Regarding "Orderly or disorderly," what do you think the "disorderly option" would be?

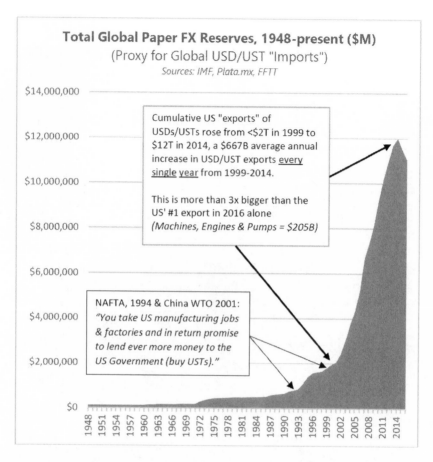

Total Global Paper FX Reserves, 1948-present ($M)
(Proxy for Global USD/UST "Imports")
Sources: IMF, Plata.mx, FFTT

Cumulative US "exports" of USDs/USTs rose from <$2T in 1999 to $12T in 2014, a $667B average annual increase in USD/UST exports every single year from 1999-2014.

This is more than 3x bigger than the US' #1 export in 2016 alone (Machines, Engines & Pumps = $205B)

NAFTA, 1994 & China WTO 2001: "You take US manufacturing jobs & factories and in return promise to lend ever more money to the US Government (buy USTs)."

Mr. X: The answer to that question ties into my earlier answer about what some forward-thinking members of Trump's cabinet see, and as the chart I showed you earlier noted, the world has stopped funding US Federal deficits for the first time in seventy years (chart as of Feb-17).

Left to its own, the "disorderly option" is catastrophic. The USD, UST yields, and LIBOR will all likely continue rising until either the US economy collapses under the weight of the USD, or the US starts World War III with either Russia, or China, or both to try to stop them from their continued and accelerating "de-dollarization."

Luke: Yikes. I bet people love you at parties….

Mr. X: Don't ask a question you don't actually want to hear the answer to, Luke! My answer might strike you as extreme, but you can't possibly be surprised by it if you are paying as close attention as I have been! For example [He pulled out a sheet of paper and read]:

> The Republicans and Democrats who make up the foreign policy elite are laying the groundwork for a more assertive US foreign policy, via a flurry of reports shaped by officials who are likely to play senior roles in a potential Clinton White House.
>
> **[Washington's foreign policy elite breaks with Obama over Syria – 10/20/16**
>
> https://www.washingtonpost.com/politics/washington-foreign-policy-elites-not-sorry-to-see-obama-go/2016/10/20/bd2334a2-9228-11e6-9c52-0b10449e33c4_story.html?utm_term=.ddb9e2e56dae]

> Putin's advisor Sergei Glaziev went as far as to officially suggest that Trump's victory saved the world from WW3. "Americans had two choices: WW3 or multilateral peace. Clinton was a symbol of war, and Trump has a chance to change this course."
>
> **[Kremlin: Clinton victory would have led to World War 3 between Russia & the US – 11/9/16**
>
> http://heatst.com/politics/kremlin-clinton-victory-would-have-led-to-world-war-3-between-russia-and-the-us/]

Luke: No, I'm not surprised; in fact, I was just recently told by a US military officer that had Clinton won, it was highly likely the US would have moved toward putting "[non-special operations] boots on the ground" in Syria, which in the aforementioned officer's estimation, would have escalated tensions between the US and Russia even further. If we look at your answer from a different angle, though, you could make the case that Trump's election could actually be a big positive, both for the US economy and globally, no?

Mr. X: US Small Business Indices certainly seem to think so. [He pointed to an article from Bloomberg.]

> **US Small Business optimism index surges by the most since 1980 – 1/10/17**
>
> [https://www.bloomberg.com/news/articles/2017-01-10/u-s-small-business-optimism-index-surges-by-most-since-1980]

Mr. X: You know what else is interesting about that 1980 date referred to in the Bloomberg story?

Luke: No, what?

Mr. X: In 1980, an actor-turned-politician and Democrat-turned-Republican got elected to the White House based partially on a promise to "Make America Great Again." [Here Mr. X pulled out a page from an old issue of *Rolling Stone Magazine* that showed Ronald Reagan's 1980 campaign button.]

Luke: Okay, now *that* is interesting...ha!

Mr. X: Indeed. Of course, there are many differences between now and 1980, but in my opinion, two such differences are absolutely critical to understand.

Luke: Which are?

Mr. X: Interest rates now versus then, and the degree of financialization/level of debt in the US economy versus levels of manufacturing then versus now.

Luke: Why are those two things so critical to understand in your opinion?

Mr. X: There seems to be a Soros/Druckenmiller-inspired trade being put on around the world that says the United States can run the same playbook it ran in 1980 or the same playbook that Germany ran in 1989.

Luke: What does that Soros/Druckenmiller playbook say?

Mr. X: It says the United States can run increasing deficits and simultaneously raise rates (loosen fiscal policy, tighten monetary policy), and in so doing, drive a stronger USD. Let me read you a passage by Druckenmiller from Jack Schwager's book *The New Market Wizards*:

> I never had more conviction about any trade than I did about the long side of the Deutsche mark when the Berlin wall came down. One of the reasons I was so bullish on the Deutsche mark was a radical currency theory proposed by George Soros in his book, *The Alchemy of Finance*. His theory was that if a huge deficit were accompanied by an

expansionary fiscal policy and tight monetary policy, the country's currency would actually rise. The dollar provided a perfect test case in the 1981-84 period. At the time, the general consensus was that the dollar would decline because of the huge budget deficit. However, because money was attracted into the country by a tight monetary policy, the dollar actually went sharply higher.

When the Berlin wall came down, it was one of those situations that I could see as clear as day. West Germany was about to run up a huge budget deficit to finance the rebuilding of East Germany. At the same time, the Bundesbank was not going to tolerate any inflation. I went headlong into the Deutsche mark. It turned out to be a terrific trade.

Luke: What's the problem with that playbook, in your opinion?

Mr. X: The short version is this: The degree of debt and financialization in the US economy are so great that the tighter monetary policy required to strengthen the USD will likely blow up the US economy before fiscal stimulus benefits accrue, forcing US deficits to widen from collapsing tax revenues instead of from accelerating productive fiscal deficits.

The longer version is that the differences now versus then are myriad:

1. The US and German Federal deficit levels in both of those cases versus the US now.
2. US and German manufacturing bases then versus the US' manufacturing base now.
3. US financialization now versus then.
4. US interest rates derivatives now versus then.

5. The reserve status of the USD now versus then (and the $9T in offshore USD debt that reserve status has driven.)

Now, to be clear, the United States could certainly *attempt* to run the playbook above that it ran in 1980 and Germany ran in 1989, but in my opinion, if the United States tries, it will likely fail, and possibly fail disastrously.

Luke: Why?

Mr. X: Because US economic financialization levels mean US tax receipts will fall as rates rise—indeed, US tax receipts are already falling year-to-year, after only what, two tiny interest rate hikes and a 100bp increase in LIBOR in twelve months? CNS News made this point on December 12, 2016:

[Mr. X turned the page in his folder and read as follows.]

> While individual income tax receipts increased y/y in the Oct-Nov period, revenues from corporate income taxes, Social Security & other taxes, excise taxes, estate & gift taxes, and customs duties all declined y/y...
>
> ...the Federal government spent $602 billion in the Oct-Nov period, thus running a deficit of $180 billion in the 1st two months of the year—despite collecting record individual income tax revenues.
>
> **[US individual income tax receipts set record for 1st 2 months of FY17, but *still* runs $180 billion deficit as total income tax receipts fall 2% y/y while Federal spending rises 6% y/y**
>
> http://www.cnsnews.com/news/article/terence-p-jeffrey/213300000000-individual-income-taxes-set-record-first-2-months-fy17]

Mr. X: As this occurs, it will lead to rising US funding needs, which, because US Federal debt levels are above 100 percent of the GDP, higher rates and a continued foreign official creditor UST buyers' strike could kick off a US BoP crisis.

Again, to be clear, I'm not saying the United States will not attempt to run the Druckenmiller/Soros playbook of loosening fiscal stimulus while simultaneously tightening monetary policy, or that such an action wouldn't drive the USD higher in the near term; it likely would were it attempted. What I'm saying is that as Hugo Salinas-Price noted, further moves to strengthen the USD will force other nations to move away from the USD at an even faster rate than they already are.

Ultimately, the differences I highlighted earlier of today versus the United States in 1980 or Germany in 1989 suggest to me that the end game must be a USD devaluation.

Luke: Couldn't the "border tax adjustment" that House Republicans have proposed actually do something semantically similar? (USD up, interest rates up, etc.)?

Mr. X: Yes, it likely could. And as I noted earlier, I think Trump knows exactly what his end game is in all this. I think he understands it could serve as a means to get to the end that got him elected—forcing the world to "change the money system" to weaken the USD to make US manufacturing competitive again, to rebalance a wildly unbalanced US economy, away from Washington, DC and back toward flyover country.

Luke: What if you're wrong?

Mr. X: If I'm wrong, then buckle up because it means the world will likely begin accelerating toward William White's "disorderly outcomes" we speculated on earlier.

Luke: Why? Why can't we just "extend and pretend" this situation for another 5-10 years?

Mr. X: Because of US Baby Boomer demographics. In the third quarter of 2016, US deficits began structurally widening as a percentage of the GDP again for the first time since 2009. Here, look at the chart. [He slid a chart over to me.] This move created an environment without any organic foreign official UST buyers. It's not a question of "When will the problem start?" It already started in the third quarter of 2014 when the world stopped sterilizing USD deficits/outflows (FX reserves peaked and began falling), and it began accelerating significantly in the third quarter of 2016, when the US Federal deficit as a percent of GDP began rising for the first time since the Great Financial Crisis. This happened because the strengthening USD and rising US rates began driving the first year-over-year decline in US Federal tax receipts since the recession.

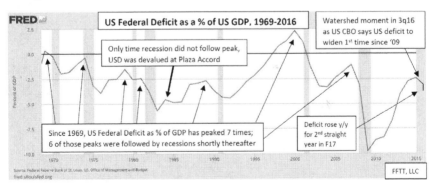

Mr. X: This means that Washington (and through the USD, the rest of the world) are now on the clock. Either...

1. The world must begin growing USD stockpiles (FX reserves) again,

2. Washington must massively cut deficits (entitlements/defense), or

3. The Fed must renew QE to provide needed USDs to the world (thus continuing the status quo).

Until one of those three are chosen, UST yields, LIBOR, and the USD will likely continue to rise (cet par), until something somewhere in the world "breaks."

Luke: Given all of this, how are you positioning your own assets?

Mr. X: As I look around the world, trying to see "the forest for the trees" as you say, here's what I see: *The "giants" in the current global "money system" are all short and/or actively shorting even more USD in very large sizes.* Global central banks? Selling USTs at a record pace. China? Dumping FX reserves at a frenetic pace while simultaneously building ghost cities, and buying commodity assets, gold, and other effective USD "short" positions. Russia? Dumping USTs and shorting USDs (USD bond deal). Saudi Arabia? Dumping FX reserves and shorting USD (USD bond deal.)

Some high-profile US academics have written articles encouraging "giants" to structurally short the USD. [He flipped the page to another article.] For example, here's what Ken Rogoff said:

> I am just proposing that emerging markets shift a significant share of the trillions of dollars in foreign-currency reserves that they now hold (China alone has official reserves of $3.3 trillion) into gold. Even shifting, say, up to 10% of their reserves into gold would not bring

them anywhere near the many rich countries that hold 60-70% of their (admittedly smaller) official reserves in gold.

Why would the system work better with a larger share of gold reserves? The problem with the status quo is that emerging markets as a group are competing for rich-country bonds, which is helping to drive down the interest rates they receive. With interest rates stuck near zero, rich-country bond prices cannot drop much more than they already have, while the supply of advanced-country debt is limited by tax capacity and risk tolerance.

Gold, despite being in nearly fixed supply, does not have this problem, because there is no limit on its price.

I don't want to create the impression that by shifting into gold, emerging markets would somehow benefit at the expense of advanced economies. After all, the status quo is that advanced-economy central banks and treasuries hold vastly more gold than emerging markets do, *and a systematic shift by emerging markets will bid up its price. But this is not a systemic problem; and, in fact, a rise in gold prices would close part of the gap between demand and supply for safe assets that has emerged due to the zero lower bound on interest rates.*

[Gold as Emerging Market reserve asset: Ken Rogoff - 5/3/16

https://www.project-syndicate.org/commentary/gold-as-emerging-market-reserve-asset-by-kenneth-rogoff-2016-05. Emphasis mine.]

Mr. X: Even Warren Buffett felt like shorting USDs would eventually be a good idea back in 2012 (and given a slant in

Berkshire's acquisitions toward real assets in recent years, arguably even before 2012):

> Most of these currency-based investments are thought of as "safe." In truth, they are among the most dangerous of assets...their risk is huge.

> "In God We Trust" may be imprinted on our currency, but the hand that activates our government's printing press has been all too human. High interest rates, of course, can compensate purchasers for the inflation risk they face with currency-based investments—and indeed, rates in the early 1980s did that job nicely. Current rates, however, do not come close to offsetting the purchasing-power risk that investors assume. Right now, bonds should come with a warning label. – Warren Buffett, Berkshire Hathaway Annual Letter, 2012

Those investors putting on the Druckenmiller/Soros strong USD trade might do well to read that Buffett quote: "Current rates do not come close to offsetting purchasing-power risk that investors assume." Translation: Rates would have to go *way* higher for the US to effectively implement in 2017E the same strategy it implemented in 1980 or that Germany implemented in 1989. As such, when I look around and see all of these giants shorting USD, one of two things seems most likely to happen to me:

1. The giants are going to cover their USD short lower (i.e., USD massively devalued – i.e., White's "orderly" outcome), or

2. The system will continue to squeeze USD higher until the giants are forced to implement a new system that will allow them to cover their shorts.

Mr. X: Implied in whether number one or two above happens is a major political change happening somewhere. I am not privy to such decision-making, so I am just using the same publicly-available information you have, but to my eyes, it certainly seems possible that such a major political change may have happened on November 8, 2016 with the election of Trump...but we shall see.

The bottom line is that, in my opinion, there is informational value to seeing so many giants shorting USD...but one must be cognizant that until the aforementioned political outcome is decided, being short, the USD will likely be "wrong"...until it no longer is.

Luke: So if shorting USD will likely be wrong until a political decision is made somewhere, why have giants been shorting USD so aggressively over the past few years?

Mr. X: Great question. There are really a few answers:

First, giants are so big that they must position well ahead of any such political announcement.

Secondly, even if they are "wrong" for a time ahead of such an announcement, they don't mark their books to market monthly, quarterly, or even annually. They are acting with a much bigger (geopolitical) mandate.

Finally, and in my opinion most importantly, neither you nor I are privy to whether such political outcomes are being discussed behind the scenes anywhere in the world, but these giants are...and they have been acting to short USD in size for the last several years...so what does that tell you?

Luke: Well, if we watch what they do rather than what they say, it should tell us that a change of the money system and/or devaluation of the USD has been being actively discussed by the giants for years, no?

Mr. X: That's my take on it.

Luke: So you're basically positioning your own personal assets for the other side of what you see as an eventual USD devaluation and/or change in the money system that drives the same outcome, and you're willing to take any pain a strong USD causes in the meantime?

Mr. X: Yes, I am…and interestingly, since last summer, US markets have been increasingly trading that way as well (industrials, energy, highly-indebted companies, etc.)

Luke: Agreed. Anything else you're doing to position for the way you're seeing things?

Mr. X: I do buy gold bullion coins whenever I get the opportunity. I buy them for me; I buy them for my kids; I buy them as gifts for my grandkids. I always buy physical bullion coins, and I never care about the price.

Luke: Never care about the price! Why not?

Mr. X: Gold has risen 30 percent in nominal USD terms in the past thirty-seven years. Do you know of any other asset class with so low a return over that time?

Luke: No, I don't, but that doesn't mean much. What if gold hasn't done anything for so long for a good reason?

Mr. X: (Smiling) Oh, there's a "good" reason why gold hasn't done anything for so long! So much ink has been spilled debating whether gold is manipulated or not, but I always thought those debates missed the forest for the trees, as you say. Just recently, I read an old US State Department cable from 1974 that confirmed my longstanding suspicions.

Luke: Confirmed what longstanding suspicions? What were your suspicions?

Mr. X: Analysts have always been so focused on debating whether gold futures were manipulated or not that they missed the forest for the trees: The gold futures market *is* the manipulation! Those aren't my words, mind you, those are the words of the US State Department. This quote came from WikiLeaks:

[Mr. X turned to his folder and read as follows.]

> To the dealers' expectations, will be the formation of a sizable gold futures market. Each of the dealers expressed the belief that the futures market would be of significant proportion and physical trading would be miniscule by comparison. *Also expressed was the expectation that large volume futures dealing would create a highly volatile market. In turn, the volatile price movements would diminish the initial demand for physical holding and most likely negate long-term hoarding by U.S. citizens.*
>
> [Source: https://wikileaks.org/plusd/cables/1974LONDON16154_b.html]

Luke: Wow…chalk another one up for the "conspiracy theorists" I guess.

Mr. X: Indeed.

Luke: I agree with you on physical gold, but why don't you care about the price you buy at?

Mr. X: To my eyes, physical gold is being moved back into the global "money system" by China, Russia, and others, and we now know that gold has been systematically undervalued by the very method used to trade it! This is why I and many like me around the world buy physical gold coins whenever we can, regardless of their USD price.

Maybe gold will never do anything (it may not for as long as the oversized USD gold futures market continues to do the job correctly envisioned for it by the US State Department per above), but if anything ever changes with the "money system" defined in part by this "gold market," and this "money system change" leads gold prices to become more "physically-driven," well…gold is currently not even priced in the correct postal code in USD terms.

Luke: And China, Russia, and others are shifting the gold market back toward being more physically-driven?

Mr. X: Yes. If they just keep doing what they're doing—"de-dollarizing" as you call it—well, I can't tell you when the gold futures market will cease dominating the pricing of physical, but I can tell you it will likely be spectacular to behold whenever it happens!

Luke: Many people have long been speculating about when the gold futures market could blow up, and to-date, they have been proven spectacularly wrong…are you saying you think the gold futures market could blow up?

Mr. X: I'm not in the predictions business—I've been running in these circles far too long…. I am simply reading the tea leaves. I remember vividly when the London Gold Pool was breaking down in the late 1960s; much that's happening today reminds me of then.

If recent physical gold flow trends from West to East continue to rhyme with what happened in the late 1960s and then through the 1970s, I don't need to get timing precisely right; I just need to be there when it happens.

Luke: What do you mean you don't need to get timing precisely right? It matters greatly to most investors!

Mr. X: Luke, you should know this: What was the price of gold in USD in the late 1960s when the London Gold Pool began breaking down?

Luke: Thirty-five dollars per ounce.

Mr. X: Correct. And what was the price of gold in USD in January 1980, by the time the breakdown of the Bretton Woods currency system had reached its denouement?

Luke: Eight hundred dollars or so per ounce.

Mr. X: Correct again. Now, if the preponderance of the evidence strongly suggests we are four years or more into the breakdown of the current USD-centric petrodollar system and that, during the last system, we saw the price of gold rise twenty-five times, why should I care about getting the timing exactly right?

Luke: But this change to the global currency system just began, didn't it? Couldn't these changes take decades to come to fruition, if they do at all?

Mr. X: These changes did not "just begin," Luke. We are not months into this trend. China was admitted to the WTO sixteen years ago. The Euro began trading eighteen years ago. The US financial system was shown to be made of "balsa wood and baby tears" eight years ago. China and Iran began transacting oil in CNY five years ago. Global FX reserves peaked and began falling nearly three years ago. China and Russia began transacting oil in non-USD nearly two years ago.

Critically, in a tell-tale sign that a US BoP crisis had begun, in the third quarter of 2016, the US Federal deficit began widening as a percentage of the GDP for the first time since 2009…that was over a year ago!

Luke: For those who don't need to worry about quarterly or annual performance mandates, I see your point—you wouldn't care.

Mr. X: Correct. The challenge for those with quarterly performance mandates is that these currency system shifts tend to move very slowly, and then all at once. That's how the last currency system breakdown happened in the late 1960s and early 1970s, and it's how the previous currency system breakdown happened as well.

Luke: Wait, what?

Mr. X: You once wrote "Arguably the most undervalued asset on Wall Street are history books." I agree wholeheartedly—check out the following excerpts from Liaquat Ahamed's *Lords of Finance: The Bankers Who Broke the World* that I mentioned to you previously:

[Mr. X pulled out a sheet of paper from his folder and read as follows.]

Page 461: On the evening of April 18 (1933), FDR gathered his economic advisers in the Red Room at the White House to discuss preparations for the forthcoming World Economic Conference in London. With a chuckle, Roosevelt casually turned to his aides and said, "Congratulate me. We are off the gold standard." Displaying the Thomas amendment to the Agricultural Adjustment Act, which gave the president the authority to devalue the USD against gold by up to 50% and to issue $3B in greenbacks without gold backing, he announced that he had agreed to support the measure.

"At that moment hell broke loose in the room," remembered Raymond Moley. Herbert Feis, the economic advisor to the State Department, looked as if he were about to throw up. Warburg and Douglas were so horrified that they began to argue with the president, scolding him as if "he were a perverse and particularly backward schoolboy." *Warburg declared that the legislation was "completely hare-brained and irresponsible" and would lead to "uncontrolled inflation and complete chaos."*

Page 462: The discussion continued until midnight. Leaving the White House, a group of aides—Warburg, Douglas, Moley, and William Bullitt, a special assistant to the secretary of state—having just been presented with what many of them viewed as the most fateful step since the war, were unable to sleep and continued the discussion in Moley's hotel room. They talked for half the night, analyzing the impact on the credibility of the whole New Deal program, the value of the dollar, capital flows and relations with other countries. *Finally, Douglas announced, "Well, this is the end of western civilization."*

But in the days after the Roosevelt decision, *as the dollar fell against gold, the stock market soared by 15%. Financial markets gave the move an overwhelming vote of confidence.* Even the Morgan bankers, historically among the most staunch defenders of the gold standard, could not resist cheering. "Your action in going off gold saved the country from complete collapse," wrote Russell Leffingwell to the president.

During the following three months, wholesale prices jumped by 45% and stock prices doubled. *With prices rising, the real cost of borrowing money plummeted.* New orders for heavy machinery soared by 100%, auto sales doubled, and overall industrial production shot up 50%.

[Emphasis mine.]

Then, as now, the orthodox economists of the day were every bit as vehemently against FDR changing the money system as Krugman, Summers, Wolfers, and others are about Trump potentially changing the money system today. History appears to be rhyming.

Interestingly, back in 2002 in what was one of his seminal speeches up until that point, Great Depression expert Ben Bernanke told the world that a USD devaluation would work in the worst case, and now that US tax receipts have begun rolling over and US deficits widening as a percentage of GDP even before fiscal stimulus starts, the worst case is here:

Although a policy of intervening to affect the exchange value of the dollar is nowhere on the horizon today, it's worth noting that there have been times when exchange rate policy has been an effective weapon against deflation.

A striking example from U.S. history is Franklin Roosevelt's 40% devaluation of the dollar against gold in 1933-34, enforced by a program of gold purchases and domestic money creation. The devaluation and the rapid increase in money supply it permitted ended the U.S. deflation remarkably quickly. Indeed, consumer price inflation in the United States, year on year, went from -10.3% in 1932 to -5.1% in 1933 to 3.4% in 1934.

The economy grew strongly, and by the way, 1934 was one of the best years of the century for the stock market. If nothing else, the episode illustrates that monetary actions can have powerful effects on the economy, even when the nominal interest rate is at or near zero, as was the case at the time of Roosevelt's devaluation.

[Ben Bernanke, "Deflation – Making Sure It Doesn't Happen Here" – 11/21/02

https://www.federalreserve.gov/boarddocs/speeches /2002/20021121/]

Luke: So what is your takeaway from those historical excerpts?

Mr. X: My takeaway is that the Fed knows a USD devaluation would work, the USD is typically the purvey of the US Treasury, and the Trump Administration seems amenable to a "weak USD" policy.

However, the status quo neoliberal economists (whose policies have in no small part gotten us into this mess) are squawking that "Trump is not particularly interested in hearing from the academic economist club." Markets seem to be starting to anticipate this.

Luke: What markets are starting to anticipate what?

Mr. X: Neoliberal economists and Western politicians have long been optimistic that they would be able to renege on the Western social entitlement promises now coming due without too severe a political cost; in my opinion, their hopes of reneging on entitlements were crushed by the 1-2 punch of Brexit and Trump.

I think Western neoliberal economists are beginning to realize there will be no entitlement reform. They are beginning to realize that every single penny owed for these entitlements will be printed and paid out. And I think "Mr. Market" is beginning to sniff this out.

In my opinion, global equity markets are beginning to sniff out the liquidity impacts of that, particularly when we look at equity markets relative to global sovereign debt markets.

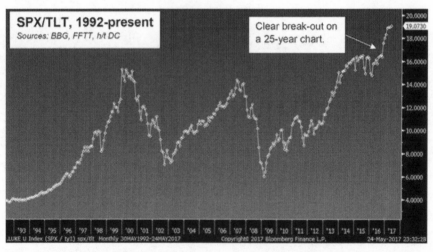

Luke: Fascinating…I agree. Thank you for your time. Let's catch up again soon.

Mr. X: I will be in touch soon. Thank you.

Chapter 4

THE FOURTH MEETING, DINNER, MAY 2017

US MILITARY AND BUSINESS LEADERS' VIEW ON A WEAKER USD AND US ECONOMIC IMBALANCES

Luke: After our first few meetings, I was left with a big question in my mind: How does "the military-industrial complex," as President Eisenhower once famously referred to it, feel about the trends you have referred to?

Mr. X: Well, it's always dangerous to overgeneralize, but what I am hearing and what I am reading suggests that at least some of the US military's leadership is in favor of a reduced global role for the US military and a rebalancing of the US economy that would likely happen with a much weaker USD.

Luke: Really? I'm more than a little surprised to hear this. Why do you think this?

Mr. X: The hints are all around for anyone willing to see things as they are.

Luke: What kinds of hints?

Mr. X: Well, for example, a recent article in the *Miami Herald*, in which the head of the US Special Forces command noted that the troops are "tired" from all the constant deployments over the past fifteen years.

[Elite US troops are being worked too hard, spread too thin, military commander warns – 5/4/17

http://www.miamiherald.com/news/nation-world/national/article148682744.html]

Luke, you're an American citizen while I'm not, so I'm sure you can tell me about the implications of the US' Special Ops leaders admitting they are tired, no?

Luke: Oh, no question—these guys are the best of the best. The best athletes from their high schools, brilliant students, often multi-lingual, big, fast, strong...the best of the best. If they are saying "We need to make a change in direction," that's a huge tell.

Mr. X: I agree. What's more, they aren't the only ones saying such things. US military leadership at the highest levels have been strongly recommending a significant change in not just military strategy, but that such a change in military strategy *requires*: a) a significant change in US economic policy that sounds like it needs a weaker USD, and b) that the US needs to make these significant changes *soon.*

In fact, the US military said the greatest threat to US National Security is US Federal debt, and by extension, US economic policies.

Luke: When did it say *that*?

Mr. X: Over five years ago.

Luke: Do you have some excerpts of exactly what it said, and where?

[Smiling, Mr. X handed over a paperback book with a sheet of paper stapled to the front cover.]

Mr. X: Now, Luke, how well do you know me? This is a copy of Edward Luce's excellent 2012 book *Time to Start Thinking: America in the Age of Descent.* I've even taken the liberty of highlighting a few quotes from the book—they are listed on the sheet of paper stapled to the front cover. Let me read them to you:

> "The window on America's hegemony is closing. We are at a point right now where we still have choices. By 2021, we will no longer have choices."

> "The US is way too dependent on its military, and should sharply reduce its 'global footprint' by winding up all wars, notably in Afghanistan, and by closing peacetime military bases in Germany, South Korea, the UK, and elsewhere…. All this is a means to an end, which is to restore America's economic vitality."

> "Our #1 goal should be to restore American prosperity. As such, we recommend the Pentagon shrink its budget by at least 20%...most of the savings would be spent on civilian priorities such as infrastructure, education and foreign aid."

> "Nobody here thinks the politics in this town are going to change overnight; all we're saying is that we're in trouble if they don't. This isn't about ideology, it is about understanding where we are as a country."

> **Conclusions of sixteen high-ranking US military officers who participated in a 2011 strategy session at the National Defense University:**

"The #1 threat facing America is its rising debt burden. [This threat] is greater than that posed by terrorism, weapons of mass destruction, and global warming.... We are borrowing money from China to build weapons to face down China. That is a broken strategy...it is a failed strategy from a national security perspective."

— Former Chairman, Joint Chiefs of Staff Admiral Michael Mullen, 2011

Mr. X: In the book, Luce interviews numerous luminaries from the US military, business, political, educational, and scientific communities. His conclusion can be easily inferred from the quote from which he sourced the title of his book. It's by Sir Ernest Rutherford, Nobel Prize-winning chemist:

> **"Gentlemen, we have run out of money. It is time to start thinking."**

Luke: Wow...so the US military's senior leadership said the United States' fiscal situation is the biggest threat to US national security...a full six years ago!

Mr. X: Yes. Undoubtedly, many readers may reflexively disagree with the assessments of the senior US military personnel, the former Chairman of the US Joint Chiefs of Staff, but they shouldn't. The logic and reasoning laid out on the front page is simply the modern version of the Asian philosopher Sun Tzu's statement in *The Art of War* oft-quoted on Wall Street:

> **"Where the army is, prices are high; when prices rise the wealth of the people is exhausted. There is no instance of a nation benefitting from prolonged warfare."**

Mr. X: When such philosophical teachings remain relevant after more than 2,000 years, it seems unlikely to me that the logic in question is faulty. Echoes of Sun Tzu's teaching above can even be heard in a modern military quote by General Robert H. Barrow, USMC:

> **"Amateurs talk about tactics, but professionals study logistics."**

Luke: So we know the US military sees the United States' fiscal and debt situation as a key weakness; any indication that potential US enemies might be aware of this weakness as well?

Mr. X: Based on my readings, it seems pretty safe to assume that not only are potential US enemies aware of the US' fiscal weaknesses, but they have been actively trying to exploit them. For example, consider this article in the *Epoch Times* from February 16, 2016. [He handed me a printed-out page]:

> **Chinese general says "Contain the US by attacking its finances"**
>
> A major general in the Chinese military is calling for China to contain the United States by attacking its finances. "That's the way to control America's lifeblood," writes Maj. Gen. Qiao Liang, a professor at the People's Liberation Army (PLA) National Defense University, in an op-ed published in China Military Online, the official mouthpiece of the PLA.
>
> "To effectively contain the United States, other countries shall think more about how to cut off the capital flow to the United States while formulating their strategies," he writes.

[http://www.theepochtimes.com/n3/1967150-chinese-general-says-contain-the-united-states-by-attacking-its-finances/]

And here's an example regarding Russia…. In October 2016, Vladimir Putin said, "The US has many such problems, more than enough. Even though it is a leading world economy, a super-power undoubtedly, but there are many unsolved problems."

"For example—the massive government debt. This is a [bomb] in slow motion—both for the US economy and the international financial system. Nobody knows what to do about it. Are they going to devalue the debt in the future? Or is there another solution? Nobody knows."

Luke: Surely China, Russia, and other nations would never actually follow such advice?

Mr. X: Yes, about that…China openly announced it would begin following that advice nearly four years ago…. I have a couple of articles here to verify that.

[He turned a page in his folder and showed them to me.]

PBOC: No longer in China's favor to boost record FX reserves (stockpile USTs) – 11/20/13

https://www.bloomberg.com/news/articles/2013-11-20/pboc-says-no-longer-in-china-s-favor-to-boost-record-reserves

US bond market's biggest buyers (Central Banks) are selling like never before – 9/25/16

https://www.bloomberg.com/news/articles/2016-09-25/u-s-bond-market-s-biggest-buyers-are-selling-like-never-before

And as we noted in our last conversations, beginning in the third quarter of 2014, global FX reserves began falling at the fastest pace in seventy years.

Luke: Which means global Central Banks began de-funding the US government a full three years ago....

Mr. X: Yes...led by China and Russia.

Luke: How the heck were China and other nations able to pull off such a move without Washington noticing?

Mr. X: It appears China, in particular, was playing "the long game" while Washington was engaged in its typical two-year election cycle:

> In 1999, when Qiao was still a colonel, he co-authored the book "Unrestricted Warfare" with another colonel, Wang Xiangsui. In "Unrestricted Warfare," Qiao and Wang promoted the use of terrorism, cyberattacks, legal warfare (also called "lawfare"), and economic warfare against the US.
>
> > **[Chinese general says "Contain the US by attacking its finances" – 2/16/16**
> >
> > http://www.theepochtimes.com/n3/1967150-chinese-general-says-contain-the-united-states-by-attacking-its-finances/]

Luke: Qiao wrote the book eighteen *years* ago, two years before China went into the WTO? And yet our political leaders still allowed China into the WTO!

Mr. X: Yes, and how about this. Listen to what Ching-Hua Wang said. She was Head of the Biotechnology Department at California State University in Camarillo in 2011 when she was quoted in Luce's book *Time to Start Thinking*:

> In China, she said, people tend to think in the long term. Americans seemingly cannot see beyond the next electoral cycle. "When I was a child [growing up in China], they had a slogan: 'Overtake the UK and catch up with the US. China is halfway there and the goal hasn't changed."

> "He talks to me about all the support government is putting into science and education in China. When I compare what is happening in China to the budget cuts we're getting in California, I feel really tempted to go back to teach in China."

This theme of the United States not having a unified strategy and politically being painfully short-sighted runs consistently throughout Edward Luce's book:

> A few months earlier, Brad Avakian [he was Oregon's Labor Commissioner at the time] had been on an official visit to Taiwan. One evening his hosts took him out for a drink. As they began to unwind, the conversation turned to America. 'These guys were literally laughing at America. They couldn't understand the game we were playing. They said "Please keep sending us all the jobs, everything else will follow."

And the frustration with US political decision-making appears to extend from the "military" to the "industrial" portion of what your President Eisenhower called the "military-industrial complex." GE CEO Jeffrey Immelt is quoted in Luce's book as saying:

> If you even whisper the phrase "industrial policy" in Washington DC today, within 24 hours you will be stoned

to death. I mean, China is out there eating [our] lunch every day but we still won't challenge the orthodoxy…. I read all these Washington economists' reports and think tank studies that say "Let the market work", except that the guys who are writing the books in China think it's f***ing bullsh*t. [They say] "Please let those guys in Washington keep reading those books. Things are going just fine!"

And former Intel CEO Andy Grove is also quoted in the book as saying:

We must abandon the attitude of "Potato chips, computer chips, what's the difference?" Without domestic plants, US-headquartered companies turn into mere wholesalers, & companies' ability to innovate tends to shift to the place where it is making its products. As DARPA (the Pentagon's R&D unit) says, "To innovate, you must make."

Luke: So I guess the $64,000 question is have you read or heard anywhere in your travels about what the US military's recommendations are for the United States to get out of this fiscal spiral?

Mr. X: Interestingly enough, yes. In *Time to Start Thinking*, Luce noted that shortly after his meeting with the sixteen senior military officers at the National Defense University (NDU), he came across an article written by two US military officers (Capt. Porter and Col. Mykleby) in *Foreign Policy* magazine entitled a "National Strategic Narrative."

I've included a link to the full "NSN" report on that front sheet stapled to the book itself:

[https://www.wilsoncenter.org/sites/default/files/A%20National%20Strategic%20Narrative.pdf]

The report at the link contains many of the same arguments (but with fewer specifics) than the NDU report quoted on the front page. Here are a few excerpts of the summary of their argument:

> Porter and Mykleby give us a non-partisan blueprint for understanding and reacting to the changes of the 21st century world. In one sentence, the strategic narrative of the US in the 21st century is that we *want to become the strongest competitor and most influential player in a deeply inter-connected global system, which requires that we invest less in defense and more in sustainable prosperity and the tools of effective global engagement.*
>
> In other words, the US should stop trying to dominate and direct global events. The best we can do is to build our capital so that we can influence events as they rise....
>
> This in turn means that the starting point for our strategy should be internal rather than external. The 2010 National Security Strategy did indeed focus on national renewal and global leadership, but this account makes an even stronger case for why we have to focus first and foremost on investing our resources domestically in those national resources that can be sustained, such as our youth and our natural resources (ranging from crops, livestock, and potable water to sources of energy and materials for industry.)
>
> **From deterrence and defense to civilian engagement and competition.** Here in many ways is the hard nub of this narrative. Chairman of the Joint Chiefs Admiral Mike Mullen has already said publicly that the US deficit is our biggest national security threat. He and Secretary of Defense Robert Gates have also given speeches and written articles calling for "demilitarizing American foreign policy" and investing more in the tools of civilian engagements—diplomacy and defense. As we modernize

our military and cut spending on the tools of 20th century warfare, we must also invest in a security complex that includes *all* domestic and foreign policy assets.

Our credibility also requires a willingness to compete with others. Instead of defeatism and protectionism, we must embrace competition as a way to make ourselves stronger and better. *A willingness to compete means a new narrative on trade and a new willingness to invest in the skills, education, energy sources, and infrastructure necessary to make our products competitive.*

From national security to national prosperity and security. The piece closes with a call for a National Prosperity and Security Act to replace the National Security Act of 1947 [Another reference to a change in the seventy-year-old post-war order]. The term "national security" only entered the foreign policy lexicon after 1947 to reflect the merger of defense and foreign affairs. Today our security lies as much or more in our prosperity as in our military capabilities. Our vocabulary, our institutions, and our assumptions must reflect that shift.

"National security" has become a trump card, justifying military spending even as *the domestic foundations of our national strength are crumbling.* "National prosperity and security" reminds us where our true security begins. [Emphasis mine]

That is a summary of Captain Porter and Colonel Mykleby's argument; what follows are excerpts of some of their exact words:

Without doubt, our greatest resource is America's young people, who will shape and execute the vision needed to take this nation forward into an uncertain future. But this may require a re-awakening, of sorts. Perhaps because our nation has been so blessed over time, many of us have forgotten that rewards must be earned, *there is no "free ride"*—that fair competition and hard work bring with them a true sense of accomplishment. We can no longer expect the ingenuity and labor of past generations to sustain our growth as a nation for generations to come. We must embrace the reality that with opportunity comes challenge, and that retooling our competitiveness requires a commitment and investment in the future.

Our first priority then, is intellectual capital and a sustainable infrastructure of education, health, and social services to provide for the continued development and growth of America's youth…. Our third investment priority is to develop a plan for the sustainable access to, cultivation and use of, the natural resources we need for our continued wellbeing, prosperity and economic growth in the world marketplace.

Fair Competition and Deterrence

Competition is a powerful, and often misunderstood, concept. *Fair competition*—of ideas and enterprises, among individuals, organizations, and nations—is what has driven Americans to achieve greatness across the spectrum of human endeavor. And yet with globalization, we seem to have developed a strange apprehension about the efficacy of our ability to apply the innovation and hard work necessary to successfully compete in a complex security and economic environment.

We cannot isolate our own prosperity and security from the global system. *Even in a land as rich as ours, we too have seen the gradual breakdown of rural communities and the rapid expansion of our cities.* We have experienced migration, crime and domestic terrorism. We struggle with joblessness and despite a low rate of illiteracy, *we are losing our traditional role of innovation dominance in leading edge technologies and the sciences.* [Emphasis mine]

Luke: I'm blown away....

Mr. X: I was too. Did you see what I saw? In Captain Porter and Colonel Mykleby's argument and echoed in the conclusions of the sixteen senior officers at the NDU, are references to:

"Fair trade."

"Fair competition."

"A new narrative on trade."

"We have to focus first and foremost on investing our resources domestically in those national resources that can be sustained, such as our youth and our natural resources."

"The domestic foundations of our national strength are crumbling."

"Even in a land as rich as ours, we too have seen the gradual breakdown of rural communities and the rapid expansion of our cities."

"Many of us have forgotten that rewards must be earned, there is no 'free ride'—that fair competition and hard work bring with them a true sense of accomplishment."

"We are losing our traditional role of innovation dominance in leading edge technologies and the sciences."

Luke: Yes, I did.... I'm just blown away.

Mr. X: I was too. As I watched your presidential election last fall from a distance, I noted that when Donald Trump said these things, many establishment pundits called his vision of America "dark."

Yet it appears the United States' own senior military leadership (which is focused on "logistics" over "tactics" and certainly focuses on "logistics" over "partisanship") could have written critical parts of the economic script that put Trump in the White House.

Why would establishment pundits be so against a message that is in many ways the same message written some six years ago, by some of the very best and brightest in the US military? The following quote by the American economist Murray Rothbard comes to mind:

> If authentic free trade ever looms on the policy horizon, there'll be one sure way to tell. The government/media/big-business complex will oppose it tooth and nail. We'll see a string of op-eds "warning" about the imminent return of the 19th century.
>
> Media pundits and academics will raise all the old canards against the free market, that it's exploitative and anarchic without government "coordination." The establishment would react to instituting true free trade about as enthusiastically as it would to repealing the income tax.

While there are a lot of things Rothbard wrote that I do not agree with, his assessment about free trade seems quite prescient these days—the establishment economists have been squealing about Trump's (and by inference, the US military's) preferred economic plan. Remember these news stories I showed you during our last meeting?

[Mr. X passed a list to me that by now had become familiar.]

Krugman says "Deficits are good" on 10/22/16, then reverses himself and says "Deficits bad" on 1/9/17

http://krugman.blogs.nytimes.com/2016/10/22/debt-diversion-distraction/

https://www.nytimes.com/2017/01/09/opinion/deficits-matter-again.html?_r=0

Summers: Trump economic plan "voodoo", "economic creationism" – 1/3
http://money.cnn.com/2017/01/04/news/economy/larry-summers-navarro-ross-voodoo/

Wolfers: Trump favors small business v. academic economists – 1/11/17

https://www.nytimes.com/2017/01/11/upshot/why-most-economists-are-so-worried-about-trump.html

Luke: I do. With this context, they are suddenly seeming much more relevant as indicators....

Mr. X: I agree, and in my mind, here's the key: The quotes from the sixteen senior military officers at the 2011 NDU session on the front page, Admiral Mullen's quotes, and Captain Porter and Colonel Mykleby's paper all point to the same thing: The highest levels of the US military establishment have understood for over five years that the United States is already in a crisis. The officers at the NDU in 2011 even gave us a date:

"By 2021, we will no longer have choices."

The year 2021 used to seem like a long way off, but it is now merely the end of Donald Trump's presidency if he is the first one-term president since George H. W. Bush. The military warned us six years ago: "The USA is on the clock."

Luke: What do you think happens in 2021?

Mr. X: [Grabbing a pen and blank sheet of paper from his briefcase near his feet.] Luke, the math is startlingly simple and can be seen in these charts. Let's run a little sensitivity analysis. Start with Federal revenues of $3.3T and grow them at a 2 percent compound annual growth rate [CAGR]. How much did they grow in fiscal year 2016?

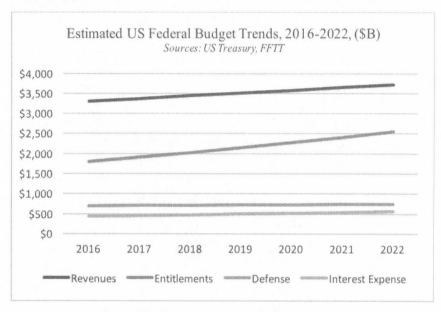

Estimated US Federal Budget Trends, 2016-2022, ($B)
Sources: US Treasury, FFTT

Luke: They were flat year to year.

Mr. X: Exactly. So let's pretend they grow 2 percent CAGR between now and 2022; critically, this assumes the United States does not have a recession between now and 2022, which would make the current economic expansion by far the longest in US history.

Then we take $1.8T in Entitlements (Medicare, Social Security) and grow them at 6 percent (growth rate in recent years). Then we take $700B in Defense and grow it 1 percent.

Finally, we take $430B in Interest Expense and add $22B per year (2 percent interest on the $1.1T per year in Federal debt the United States has added annually on average for the past ten years.) Critically, this assumes that US borrowing rates do not rise.

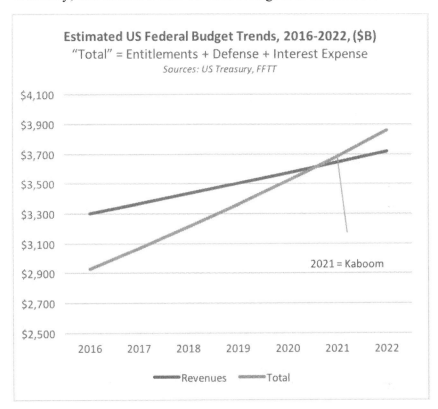

When you total those three factors (Entitlements, Defense, Interest Expense) and then graph it against US revenues projected above, you get this next chart:

The year 2021 is when the United States will be running a $200B deficit just to pay for Entitlements, Defense, and Interest Expense. It includes *none* of the other Federal government spending that the United States is currently spending an additional ~$2.2T (~11 percent of US GDP) on.

Luke: Oh, my God….

Mr. X: Yes…'Oh, my God' is right.

At this point, it should be clear why Admiral Mullen said in 2010 that the greatest threat to US National Security was not terrorism, weapons of mass destruction, or global warming, but the US Federal debt, and why the NDU study pegged 2021 as the date when the United States "will no longer have choices."

Furthermore, as I pointed out earlier, it would appear that Admiral Mullen's counterparts in China are also well aware of this math. China (nor any other nation) does not need to do anything—all it needs to do is bide its time for the next four years and let compounding math work its magic. As was said in the "Chinese general" article earlier: "To effectively contain the United States, other countries shall think more about how to cut off the capital flow to the United States while formulating their strategies."

Luke: China and Russia know they don't have to go to war with the US to win…all they have to do is avoid going to war with the US and let the magic of compounding interest do its job. The US cannot afford both its military at current spending levels and its entitlement obligations at future-promised levels for very much longer.

Mr. X: No, they cannot, and everyone knows it…well, everyone except the American people and most Western investors who are hyper-focused on short-term trading moves.

Luke: What do you mean everyone knows it?

Mr. X: If you've been paying close enough attention to the news, there have been plenty of hints. For example, the US Congress knows it. Here's a quote from CNS News from February 25, 2015:

> "The first point I want to get across is that our nation is broke," Kotlikoff testified. "Our nation's broke, and it's not broke in 75 years or 50 years or 25 years or 10 years. It's broke today. "Indeed, it may well be in worse fiscal shape than any developed country, including Greece," he said.
>
> **[Economist testifies to US Senate Budget Committee that US in worse fiscal shape than Greece**
>
> http://www.cnsnews.com/news/article/barbara-hollingsworth/economist-tells-congress-us-may-be-worse-fiscal-shape-greece]

Mr. X: Judging by comments two years ago by Alan Greenspan, former Dallas Fed Chair Richard Fisher, and former Fed Governor Larry Lindsay at the 2015 Peterson Institute on May 19, 2015, we can all but infer that the Fed knows it:

> **Richard Fisher (RF):** "In 2015E, Federal debt is $18T and that does not include Medicare, Medicaid or Social Security obligations, nor other Federal obligations such as FNM & FRE."
>
> "CBO estimates interest expense and healthcare expenditures will soon be > 50% of revenues; at some

point, you have to pay the piper." "We [the Fed] have been suppressing the yield curve—if rates rise, it's a ticking time bomb."

"Debt held by public, if you multiply that by a big number you get total US off-balance sheet liabilities. The Fed has taken out the urgency to finance those liabilities by suppressing the yield curve, but we cannot continue to count on the Central Bank underwriting the government."

"Imagine the political turmoil if you have to cut payments to those you promised and say we still have to pay interest? Both the US political right and left will both ask—well who owns our debt? It's China, Japan, etc. This is a political train wreck that is about to happen, we have to urgently come to grips with it."

Larry Lindsay (LL): "[T]he Social Security Disability fund has been cash flow negative for the past 3 years, meaning we're running down the Trust balances. That trust will be exhausted in the late 2020's...current law says that when that happens, all recipients will see benefits cut by 27%...

"Unfunded Social Security and Medicare/Medicaid liabilities when added together to US Federal debt take US obligations closer to 300% v. 100%, which is more than Greece's debt."

"The financial arrangements of the state are no longer sustainable...it is not a pretty change if we get there, and it is a matter of political liberty because government will NOT voluntarily let itself go out of business...it will use all its powers available to government to fund itself. By the way, this always ends this way—Rome, the Ming Dynasty,

Zimbabwe…it's so depressing. It always, always, always ends this way, this end game we're all talking about."

Alan Greenspan (AG): "The term Social Security "Trust Fund" is nonsense…it is a mandatory outlay and there is a 0% chance that outlay will not get made. When the fund runs out, there is no chance anything will change. The US has committed to pensions it cannot pay. We're not getting like Greece, we're getting like Illinois."

"Long term productivity has slowed, this has driven entitlements from 4.7% of US GDP in 1965 to 14.7% of GDP now. If productivity kept improving, it would keep increasing living standards and wages. We need to shrink entitlements back as a % of the pie, and we need to resolve it before we have a crisis."

"Unfortunately though, I don't see how we are going to get out of this."

"Paying for the Past" – 2015 Peterson Institute Fiscal Summit – 5/19/15

https://www.youtube.com/watch?v=pfpEHwARhvc

Mr. X: Judging by a speech that former BIS and (current OECD Economic Committee Chairman) William White gave back in October 2016, we can also infer that both the EU and the BIS know it:

The last bullet here is that our macro tools are all used up. There is very little room on the monetary side, I think. On the fiscal side, when I talk about the debt levels having ratcheted up, it is important to note that a lot of it over the course of the years has been government debt levels—

particularly in the advanced market economies. They have basically been using up their fiscal room to maneuver at the same pace as the central banks have been using their monetary room to maneuver.

I am going to tell a less pleasant story. That is that we get an assumed slowdown or a global recession…but in countries that started off with a very bad fiscal situation, there is a lot of history that indicates that a slowdown, when a country faces a very bad fiscal situation, leads to still more recourse to the central bank and to people, ordinary people and traders, seeing the writing on the wall that central bank financing will eventually lead to inflation. Everybody says: "I am out of here." There is a currency collapse and hyperinflation. We have seen it many times in history in the worst of the worst-case scenarios.

[Ultra-Easy Money—Digging the Hole Deeper? William White, October 2016, in Singapore

www.lbma.org.uk/assets/blog/alchemist_articles/Alch84Complete.pdf]

Luke: Wow….

Mr. X: Wow, indeed. Virtually everybody who matters appears to know that "something wicked this way comes," and critically, the US military thinks we have until 2021 at the latest until we start to run out of options. I suspect this is why a former BIS official fears that in the next crisis, traders may not flood into USDs for safety.

Luke: So how does this play out?

Mr. X: As we noted earlier, the best and brightest in the US military have been thinking and writing about it for years…and it sounds an awful lot like big parts of Trump's economic plan. The US military echoed sentiments Trump repeatedly stated on the campaign trail: That the US needs to engage in "fair trade," needs a "new narrative on trade," needs to "focus first and foremost on reinvesting domestically," should reconsider military alliances and expenditures, and needs to realize there is no more "free ride."

Luke: Fair enough, but how can this be engineered? How will this outcome be achieved?

Mr. X: With a weak enough USD, it can be achieved quite easily.

Luke: How?

Mr. X: Remember, the deal under the USD-centric post-war order was: "The US exports USDs to the world, and the world lends those USDs back to the US government (to provide Pax Americana) and to US consumers (to buy goods from the world.)" In short, the deal was "You take our USDs, jobs, and factories, and then lend us the money to buy your goods."

Luke: Okay, I'm with you so far...go on.

Mr. X: However, since the third quarter of 2014, the world has stopped stockpiling FX reserves for the first time in seventy years, as I've mentioned before.

[He pulled out a chart on Global Paper FX Reserves.]

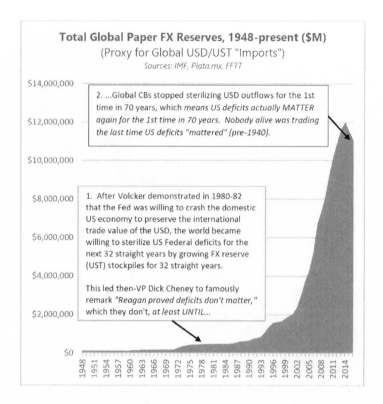

Total Global Paper FX Reserves, 1948-present ($M)
(Proxy for Global USD/UST "Imports")
Sources: IMF, Plata.mx, FFTT

2. ...Global CBs stopped sterilizing USD outflows for the 1st time in 70 years, which means US deficits actually MATTER again for the 1st time in 70 years. Nobody alive was trading the last time US deficits "mattered" (pre-1940).

1. After Volcker demonstrated in 1980-82 that the Fed was willing to crash the domestic US economy to preserve the international trade value of the USD, the world became willing to sterilize US Federal deficits for the next 32 straight years by growing FX reserve (UST) stockpiles for 32 straight years.

This led then-VP Dick Cheney to famously remark "Reagan proved deficits don't matter," which they don't, at least UNTIL...

Not many on Wall Street understand the implications of this chart because they've never had to before.

Luke: Why not?

Mr. X: Because it had never gone any direction except up for seventy years. It was a one-way chart, so who needs to understand what might happen if it fell.

Luke: Okay, so through your lens, what does the drop in global FX reserves mean?

Mr. X: In essence, the chart shows that the world is saying to the US "The prior (USD-centric) deal is off."

Luke: That seems like a pretty big deal.

Mr. X: Oh, it's not just "a pretty big deal"…it's the biggest deal! Once global FX reserves began falling, the US faced a choice: It could go to war to force the world to begin stockpiling FX reserves again, or it could change the deal. While most US citizens don't seem to be aware of it, in my eyes, it appears Hillary Clinton was preparing to take the former tact as outlined in *The Washington Post* on October 20, 2016:

> The Republicans and Democrats who make up the foreign policy elite are laying the groundwork for a more assertive US foreign policy, via a flurry of reports shaped by officials who are likely to play senior roles in a potential Clinton White House.
>
> **[Washington's foreign policy elite breaks with Obama over Syria**
>
> https://www.washingtonpost.com/politics/washington-foreign-policy-elites-not-sorry-to-see-obama-go/2016/10/20/bd2334a2-9228-11e6-9c52-0b10449e33c4_story.html?utm_term=.ddb9e2e56dae]

And listen to this opinion from the website heatst.com:

> Putin's advisor Sergei Glaziev went as far as to officially suggest that Trump's victory saved the world from WW3. "Americans had two choices: WW3 or multilateral peace. Clinton was a symbol of war, and Trump has a chance to change this course."
>
> **[Kremlin: Clinton victory would have led to World War 3 between Russia & the US – 11/9/16**
>
> http://heatst.com/politics/kremlin-clinton-victory-would-have-led-to-world-war-3-between-russia-and-the-us/]

Luke: But now, with the election of Trump, you think the US is taking a different, more nuanced strategy?

Mr. X: It certainly appears that way to me; doesn't it to you? The strategy was clearly laid out by the US military some six years ago: "The deal was you take our USDs, our jobs, and our factories and then lend us the money to buy your goods. If you are going to stop taking our USDs, then the deal is off. *We are going to take back the factories and the jobs.*"

Luke: Let's say for sake of argument you're right…. How will this happen?

Mr. X: It's quite simple. Now, note that I said "simple" but not necessarily "easy." The United States must simply devalue the USD significantly, allowing US industry to compete on its own merits for the first time in at least forty-four years and more like seventy years. Game, set, match…the United States will suddenly begin "winning" again broadly in global trade…just like President Trump wants.

Luke: Yes, but that sounds like industrial policy or socialism, doesn't it?

Mr. X: A Google exec, Vint Cerf, had an interesting comment about that exact thing in Edward Luce's book:

> A huge proportion of today's most critical technologies were born at DARPA (the Pentagon's R&D unit), among them GPS technology, the Internet, stealth technology, and the computer mouse…without the long-term support of the Pentagon, the Internet would not exist.

If DARPA had withdrawn support in 1980, we would have had no Internet. The private sector would not have had the patience or the firepower to fill DARPA's shoes.

Luke: So in your mind, how does it all go down, or how could it all go down?

Mr. X: Well, let's take a step back and look at what we have. On one side, we have the US military, the US banking system, the global banking system, the US economy, and global EM corporations and nations that have borrowed in USDs.

On the other side, we have the status quo that has benefitted massively from "the USD export trade" of the past 44-70 years: certain Washington interests (that either don't realize or care how dire the United States' fiscal situation is), USD debt merchants (that don't realize that without a much weaker USD *soon*, the USD-denominated debt they currently hold on their balance sheets as assets may be rendered worth much less—or even worthless—in the next crisis), the portions of EM nations and companies that rely on exports to the US for a living, and many neoliberal economists (many of whose self-worth is heavily tied up in the status quo system.)

Luke: Fair enough. So how do you weight the two sides?

Mr. X: Well, as I look at it, to one side are the people with all the guns and most of the money, and to the other side are the people who like the old way of doing things but don't realize that the old way of doing things in the global currency system must change one way or another, either "the easy way" or "the hard way."

Luke: So which of the groups above do you think will win out?

Mr. X: History *strongly* suggests betting on the people with all the guns and most of the money. If they want the USD to be devalued, it is going to be devalued.

Luke: Makes sense. Knowing that then, what is "the easy way" and what is "the hard way"?

Mr. X: The "easy way" is to allow President Trump to do what he says he is going to do: Devalue the USD and bring jobs and factories back to the United States. Mechanically, this could be done numerous ways. The "hard way" would be what William White laid out again in October—do nothing until the world enters a new recession, at which point the world could see "currency collapse and hyperinflation" (his words, not mine).

One way or another, the USD must be forced lower. A large amount of circumstantial evidence suggests the US defense establishment as well as numerous US multinational business elites understand that it is now a matter of national security that the USD is devalued, significantly.

The reality is that a major USD devaluation will likely entail a global currency system restructuring. We have repeatedly noted that this reworking of the global currency system appears to have been underway for much of the past decade, per comments by Vice President Mike Pence and former World Bank Chief Robert Zoellick.

Since the people with all the guns and most of the money seem to understand the situation's urgency, we remain optimistic that a USD devaluation will be moved toward, perhaps sooner than most think (especially since big changes are best done early in new presidential terms). After all, as Larry Summers noted when interviewed in Luce's *Time to Start Thinking*, quoting Winston Churchill:

"America will always do the right thing…after exhausting all the alternatives."

Given William White's recent admonitions that the world is out of maneuvering room on both the monetary and fiscal side, we remain optimistic that with all options exhausted, "the right thing" will be done (the USD devalued and the global monetary system changed).

Chapter 5

THE FIFTH MEETING, DINNER, MAY 2017

A POTENTIALLY WORSENING OUTLOOK FOR THE US DOLLAR IN THE AFTERMATH OF FRENCH ELECTIONS

Luke: Thank you for joining me, Mr. X. It's great to see you again. First, I'd like to ask you your take on the topic that is probably on everyone's minds: the outcome of the French election?

Mr. X: You're welcome; thank you for hosting me at dinner tonight. I must say, my initial thought was that the immediate existential downside risk to the EUR would seem to be mitigated for now. If anything, I think the outcome of the French election may potentially be a significant negative catalyst for the USD.

Luke: Why do you say that?

Mr. X: Well, as you have noted in your work, the USD's fundamentals have been steadily deteriorating since the third quarter of 2016. I've talked to a number of traders who saw those deteriorating USD fundamentals but were afraid to short the USD from fear the EUR could blow up post-French elections.

With the outcome of the French election now decided, the existential risk to the EUR seems to be mitigated for the time being, which in turn makes it possible that the weak USD fundamentals you've been writing about since the third quarter of 2016 may start to matter.

Luke: I've heard the same thing a number of times: "Luke, I hear you on the USD, but I cannot be short USD ahead of the possibility of Le Pen winning the French election."

Mr. X: Exactly…and Le Pen just lost, removing that existential EUR risk in the near term…and USD fundamentals are still worsening. Potentially, an interesting set-up for the USD in the back half of 2017, no?

Luke: When you say "Interesting set-up for the USD in the back half of 2017," you mean shorting the USD?

Mr. X: Yes. Based on my conversations, consensus on the USD, EUR, and CNY appears to be that they are all racing toward a cliff, with the EUR and CNY running neck-and-neck for the lead and "the cleanest dirty shirt," the USD, way behind.

Luke: We agree, but how do you see things differently?

Mr. X: Even before the French election, I thought the USD was closest to "going over the cliff," with the CNY in close second and the EUR a distant third; however, I was cognizant that the French election could have changed that order radically, but now we know it did not—the French election suggests to me that the pace at which the EUR is heading toward the cliff just slowed meaningfully. The race is now between the USD and CNY, and to my eyes, the USD is pulling away.

Luke: Interesting...that is a very contrarian view. Why do you think the USD runs into trouble before the CNY?

Mr. X: Structural factors for each that virtually no one is talking about, yet. I suspect because it is still inconvenient to talk about them.

Luke: What structural factors are you referring to?

Mr. X: Let's take the structural factors for each country separately, starting with China: Not that long ago, many were highlighting that China would soon burn down FX reserves below a critical threshold, touching off a Chinese Balance-of-Payments (BoP) crisis. That is the first structural factor: It appears that the second half 2017E Chinese BoP crisis has been delayed, as the rate of Chinese FX reserve outflows have not just slowed, they've reversed. Here's what the *Wall Street Journal* said on May 7, 2017:

> Some economists attributed April's increase to a USD that lost some ground after President Donald Trump said the U.S. currency "is getting too strong." The value of other currencies in China's reserve hoard—including the EUR, the GBP & JPY—played a significant role in the rise, said Yan Ling, an economist with China Merchants Securities.
>
> Also contributing to the reserve accumulation are the tight controls on capital outflows that the central bank began ratcheting up late last year to defend a weakening CNY, some economists said. Policymakers have been pushing harder on that lever instead of burning through the FX reserve stockpile to prop up the CNY, the economists said.
>
> **[China FX reserves rise for 3rd straight month**

https://www.wsj.com/articles/chinas-foreign-exchange-reserves-continue-to-expand-1494129841]

Luke: So China tightened capital controls, which led to a slowing and even reversal in Chinese FX reserve declines. Isn't this just a temporary phenomenon?

Mr. X: Maybe. That remains to be seen. In the meantime, China continues to lower its FX reserve needs structurally and permanently, a fact the Western mainstream financial media continues to ignore.

Luke: How is China structurally and permanently lowering its FX reserve needs?

Mr. X: It's accelerating the pace at which it's gaining the ability to print CNY for critical imports, the most critical of which, of course, are oil and gas.

Luke: How is it gaining the ability to print CNY for critical imports?

Mr. X: As you noted, China has effectively reopened the Bretton Woods gold window, through CNY in Shanghai. In just the last month, China has made another enormous stride toward gaining the ability to print CNY for oil, expanding the CNY-centric Bretton Woods system to Dubai, having already established direct trading between CNY and the Saudi riyal and the UAE dirham last fall.

[Mr. X passed me a sheet of paper with the following articles listed for reference before he continued.]

Dubai starts trading of CNY-denominated Shanghai gold futures – 4/10/17

http://www.tradearabia.com/news/BANK_323140.html

China allows CNY direct trading with Saudi riyal, UAE dirham – 9/23/16

http://news.xinhuanet.com/english/2016-09/23/c_135709142.htm

Of course, China's Dubai moves are merely the latest important step in an ongoing process that began accelerating three years ago.

[He pointed at three specific articles on the page.]

Russia, China sign historic deal to bypass USD in trade – 5/20/14

http://america.aljazeera.com/articles/2014/5/20/russia-china-bankdeal.html

China starts SGEI 11 days early for CNY gold trade, settlement – 9/18/14

http://www.reuters.com/article/us-china-gold-contract-idUSKBN0HB17F20140916

HK/SGEI link-up launches on July 10, 2015 with the explicit goal of opening China's capital account thru gold

http://hkmb.hktdc.com/en/1X0A2VVK/hktdc-research/Shanghai-Hong-Kong-Gold-Connect-Starts-on-10-July

Furthermore, China recently announced plans to expand the CNY oil market significantly in the next 2-4 months:

China plans launch of CNY oil futures in 2H17E, within 3-5 months – 4/18/17

http://af.reuters.com/article/energyOilNews/idAFL3N1HF3
RR

All of China's efforts on this front are being supported by the physical volumes moving through Shanghai, and by extension, Hong Kong. Withdrawals on the Shanghai Gold Exchange (SGE) were a massive 555 tons in the first quarter of 2017. That is a run rate of 2,220 tons, or roughly 80 percent of global gold mine supplies…and yet not a single mainstream financial media service even mentioned it. Only the website bullionstar.com notes it:

Gold withdrawals on SGE a massive 555 tons (80%+ of global gold mine supplies) in 1q17 – 5/1/17

https://www.bullionstar.com/blogs/gold-market-charts/gold-market-charts-april-2017/

It's fascinating, isn't it? China buys up more than 80 percent of the world's gold supplies in the first quarter of 2017, gold prices barely rise, and Bloomberg, Reuters, and the *Wall Street Journal* don't breathe a word of it. But China bids up the world's avocado supplies and the Western mainstream financial press is all over it…. I smell a Pulitzer here for this groundbreaking work on Chinese avocado demand!

[Laughing, he handed me a sheet listing articles on avocado imports.]

Avocado imports soar as China develops taste for 'butter fruit' – Financial Times, 4/19/17

https://www.google.com/amp/s/amp.ft.com/content/97340c8a-2652-11e7-8691-d5f7e0cd0a16

Avocado Prices Are Skyrocketing – Bloomberg News, 4/28/17

https://www.bloomberg.com/news/articles/2017-04-28/guacamole-costs-to-jump-as-avocado-shortage-sparks-record-prices

Avocado prices soar amid high demand – Fox News, 5/4/17

http://www.foxnews.com/food-drink/2017/05/03/avocado-prices-soar-amid-high-demand.html

All joking aside, there is one development I don't fully understand—China's official gold reserves have not changed for six straight months, after rising inexorably for the prior eighteen. Why? Are they signaling something? Are they lying about their levels of purchasing? Are they making room for CNY-denominated trading partners to buy physical gold (Russian purchases in particular continue to be extremely strong). Reuters notes it here:

Chinese official gold reserves unchanged for 6th straight month in April – 5/7/17

http://www.reuters.com/article/china-economy-gold-idUSL4N1I9024

Luke: What do you make of the flat-lining of Chinese official gold purchases for the past six months?

Mr. X: I don't know. I suspect we'll know when the time comes, but in the meantime, in the context of all else I've described, I'm not sure it matters.

Luke: How can you say that?

Mr. X: Because as long as China continues to make progress toward expanding the "CNY gold window" globally, it will continue gaining the ability to print CNY for oil, structurally and permanently reducing its FX reserve needs, and defunding the US government.

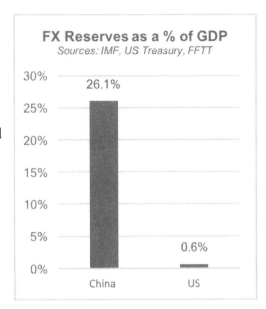

Or, as is shown in this elegantly-simplistic chart [He slid it over to me], China will gradually be able to reduce its FX reserves as a percentage of GDP from its current 26 percent level, toward the US' 0.6 percent of GDP over time.

Luke: I agree. Very few investors are watching this development.

Mr. X: That so few investors are watching is all the more fascinating because China's moves to print CNY for oil have had pronounced impacts on a variety of major global markets since the third quarter of 2014.

Luke: Such as?

Mr. X: Would you agree with my assessment that two of the most consistent "consensus trades" over the past eighteen months or so have been:

1. USD oil is going to rise to $60 or more, and;
2. CNY/USD is going lower; China needs to devalue.

Luke: Yes, I would agree. What's your point?

Mr. X: Tell me, Luke, if a greater share of the global oil market is being priced in CNY, how can USD oil rise and CNY/USD simultaneously fall?

Luke: That's a great point. If more oil's priced in CNY, then oil will probably struggle to rise sustainably unless CNY rises against the USD, no?

Mr. X: That's what I think. While few investors seem to be considering this logic, it appears physical oil markets are being made to think about it since they seem to be falling all over themselves to ship oil to Asia.... Check out these charts.

[He passed me four of them, reflecting oil shipments.]

China surpasses U.S. as world's biggest crude importer

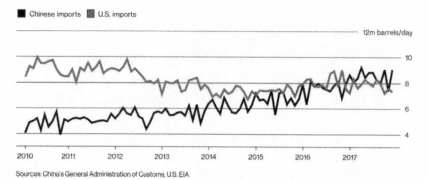

Sources: China's General Administration of Customs, U.S. EIA

It makes sense that the physical oil market is shipping to Asia, given this headline from this morning:

Almost All Oil Demand Growth in Next 25 Years to Come from Asia: Saudi Oil Min - Bloomberg, 5/8/17

It seems to me as if China has a lot of the leverage in this game, no?

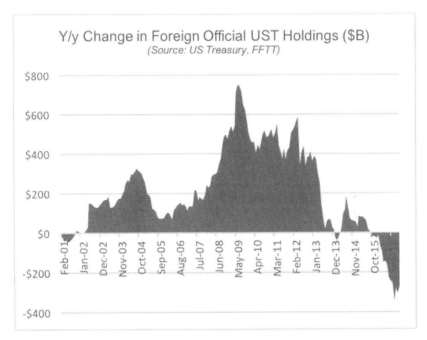

Luke: Agreed. So if you will, can you segue into how this information informs your view of the USD?

Mr. X: I'd be happy to. It's simple: China and Russia are using the combination of 1) *Their position as the world's biggest energy importer and exporter respectively*, and 2) *Reopening the Bretton Woods gold window through CNY* to gain their independence from the USD, aided by Iran and others. Their moves are forcing the dishoarding of USTs by Central Banks globally out of preference or necessity.

Luke: Go on...

Mr. X: Historically, when EMs have tried to gain their monetary and political independence from the USD, the US has "weaponized" the USD to bring them to heel. Now, it's typically not talked about out loud in polite circles on Wall Street, but we can infer that all the major players in this game understand this because they have all *explicitly* stated it.

Former senior US Treasury official Juan Zarate, in his 2013 book *Treasury's War*, notes that:

> The dollar serves as the global reserve currency and the currency of choice for international trade, and New York has remained a core financial capital and hub for dollar-clearing transactions. *With this concentration of financial and commercial power comes the ability to wield access to American markets, American banks, and American dollars as financial weapons.*

> Treasury's power ultimately stems from the ability of the US to use its financial powers with global effect. This ability, in turn, stems from the centrality and stability of New York as a global financial center, the importance of the USD as a reserve currency, and the demonstration effects, regulatory or otherwise, taken by the US in the broader international system. *If the US economy loses its predominance, or the USD sufficiently weakens, our ability to wage financial warfare could wane.*

And here's how Russia is responding, as expressed by Putin's top economic advisor, Sergey Glaziev, in a recent article:

> "America's aggression around the world is rooted in its aspiration to preserve US hegemony when they have already yielded economic leadership to China," he said.

"The United States has no tools to make all others use the dollar other than a truncheon. That is why they are indulging in a hybrid war with the entire world to shift their debt burden on to other countries, to confine everyone to the dollar and weaken territories they cannot control."

"The more aggressive the Americans are the sooner they will see the final collapse of the dollar as the only way for the victims of American aggression to stop this aggression is to get rid of the dollar. As soon as we and China are through with the dollar, it will be the end of the United States' military might," Sergey Glaziev said in an interview with TASS.

"...as it always happens when a global leader is changed, the war is for control over rimland nations. During WWI and WWII, Britain acted as an instigator in a bid to keep its global leadership. Now the US is doing the same...."

[Kremlin advisor reveals 'cure for US aggression': 'Russia & China getting rid of the USD' – 3/21/17

http://tass.com/politics/942643]

And here is China's response, as described on the website chinascope.com:

In April, Qiao Liang, a People's Liberation Army (PLA) Major-General, gave a speech at a book study forum of the Chinese Communist Party's (CCP's) Central Committee and government office. Qiao is the PLA strategist who co-authored the book, "Unrestricted War."

In his speech, Qiao explained that he has been studying finance theories and concluded that the U.S. enforces the dollar as the global currency to preserve its hegemony over the world. The U.S. will try everything, including war, to maintain the dollar's dominance in global trading. He also discussed China's strategy, to rise as a super power, amid the U.S.'s containment.

[China PLA Strategist: The US uses the USD to dominate the world – April 2017

http://chinascope.org/archives/6458/76]

Luke: OK, so we can safely infer that all the major players in the game understand the strategy of the historically-dominant player in the game, the United States. Historically, this hasn't mattered. The United States has simply been able to impose its will on all-comers. Why does this matter now, and how does that translate to your outlook for the USD?

Mr. X: You are correct to say that "Historically, it hasn't mattered." However, a look at the evidence strongly suggests it matters now!

As the aforementioned US, Russian, and Chinese authorities noted, historically, the United States strengthens the USD until EMs "break," covering their USD short in a violent risk-off episode. Once that happens, the USD strength filters back into the US economy, driving a sharp drop in US government tax receipts that the Fed addresses by lowering interest rates and/or otherwise weakening the USD to restart the entire game, with the United States comfortably back on top of the system.

Here's the thing, though: For the first time in at least thirty-five years, US government Treasury receipts are falling *before* the United States has gotten the key EMs in question (China and Russia) to "break"! Look at this chart.

[Mr. X dug in his folder and pulled out another chart.]

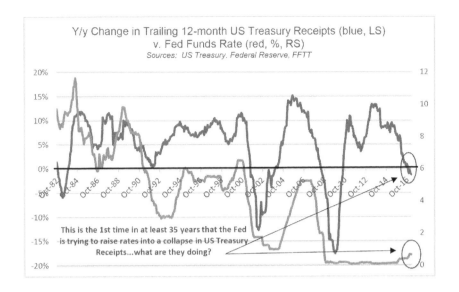

Y/y Change in Trailing 12-month US Treasury Receipts (blue, LS) v. Fed Funds Rate (red, %, RS)
Sources: US Treasury, Federal Reserve, FFTT

This is the 1st time in at least 35 years that the Fed is trying to raise rates into a collapse in US Treasury Receipts...what are they doing?

Mr. X: I just laid out the evidence that China and Russia have not only weathered the USD's best punches, but they are now accelerating their efforts to move away from the USD. At the same time, it is the US government (not China or Russia) that is seeing its funding choked off by the Fed's efforts to strengthen the USD!

Investors have never seen the game turn this way...the game has done a 180-degree turn from the script of the early 1980s in Latin America, the late 1990s in Asia and Russia, and again in 2008 with Russia, but investors are still blindly following the same script for the USD!

Luke: So how does this inform your view of the USD?

Mr. X: The old script the United States used to follow was that it would tighten USD liquidity until another nation that couldn't print USD essentially broke on the rocks of the strong USD. Historically, that was an EM or EM region, but as a practical matter, it could be anyone.

Here was the key: The USD merely had to ensure it was not the first currency over the cliff. If any other nation went over the cliff first, it would trigger a flood into USDs for safety, and the USD's hegemony would be maintained and restored.

Luke: Go on….

Mr. X: Understanding this, to my eyes, it appears that China and Russia have not only successfully weathered a "strong USD attack," but they are now actively increasing their defenses against all future attacks, using gold and their positions as the world's largest energy importer and exporter respectively.

Additionally, to my eyes, the French election has, for the time being, removed the existential threat of a rapid EUR collapse. The EUR still has issues, to be sure, but they are not as severe as what detractors would say, and at the very least, they no longer appear to be an immediate threat.

Of the "Big Three," that leaves the USD, which in my view is now thrust firmly into first place, in the race toward the cliff. The US is already seeing a decline in Treasury receipts, consumer delinquencies are rising, and oil prices have fallen rapidly in recent weeks, which should, in time, affect the resurgent US energy sector negatively given its continued position as the world's highest marginal cost producer.

All of this will likely contribute to a continuing increase in US government deficits and, therefore, Federal borrowing…but as a result of China and Russia's actions (and the launch of the EUR in 1999), the foreign official sector is no longer funding the US government on net. The US will either have to cut Federal spending (which at 22 percent of GDP will initially make the problem worse, not better), or have the Fed reimplement massive QE and/or devalue the USD.

Luke: So where is this heading?

Mr. X: [Reaches into his coat pocket and takes out a pen.] Let's talk through it…. If US deficits rise, but foreign Central Banks aren't stockpiling USTs as FX reserves anymore, then the global private sector must fund growing US deficits…. It's laid out beautifully in this chart. [He pulled out a chart from his folder and passed it to me.]

The US Federal government has an epic funding problem for the first time in fifty years. The problem began as soon as global Central Banks (CBs) stopped net buying USTs, but the USD was still only the second ugliest currency until the French election removed the near-term risk of EUR collapse, just yesterday.

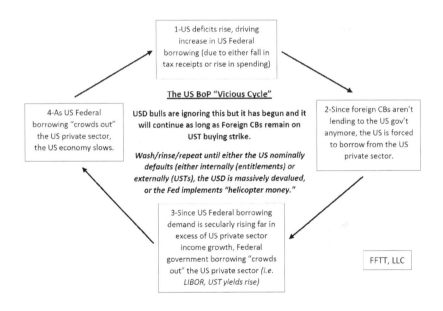

Luke: What do you expect to be the next near-term outcome of this?

Mr. X: The Fed is facing quite a dilemma: It could admit defeat, reverse course, and devalue the USD. That would go a long way toward rebalancing and fixing the world, but it would involve the Fed effectively admitting that its entire post-2008 experiment had failed.

Luke: A cursory understanding of politics and hubris would seem to suggest that won't be the option then. What's the Fed's other option?

Mr. X: Agreed. The Fed's other option is simply to fire the only weapon it has left—try to raise rates as aggressively as possible to keep the USD strong and the global private sector interested in buying what is mathematically certain to be a growing amount of USTs.

Luke: What's the catch with that option?

Mr. X: Remember, the US Federal government's tax receipts are already falling year-to-year. Raising rates into falling year-to-year US Treasury receipts is unlikely to win Federal Reserve Chairwoman Janet Yellen many friends in the White House, a White House that has already been fairly vocal both about its desire to run deficits and its desire not to have the Fed get in its way.

Luke: So you think the Fed must choose between either blowing up its remaining credibility or having its employees lose their jobs?

Mr. X: Yes, I do.

Luke: Which will it choose?

Mr. X: What is it they say about the difference between "involved" and "committed"? The chicken is "involved" with breakfast, but the pig is "committed"?

Well, in my opinion, the Fed is "committed" to interest rate hikes. I would expect that the issues we discussed here today mean the Fed will be as aggressive as possible with both jawboning and actual rate hikes in the hope that it somehow gets itself out of this jam. It likely won't work, but it appears to be all it has left. It is, as I believe you say in American football, a "Hail Mary"?

Luke: Wow…why don't we stop it there for today. Thanks again for your time, Mr. X.

Mr. X: Thank you. I look forward to speaking again soon.

Chapter 6

THE SIXTH MEETING, COFFEE, JUNE 2017

WHERE DO WE GO FROM HERE?

After taking a few weeks to digest our conversation, review my notes, and organize my thoughts, I scheduled a follow-up meeting with Mr. X to tie up some loose ends and get his thoughts on where he thought things might go from that point.

As it happened, he was going to be back in New York again, so I flew out from Cleveland again to see him. It was a beautiful late spring day in Manhattan, and we agreed to meet for coffee. I grabbed a coffee from a Starbucks near Grand Central Station and walked to Bryant Park, behind the New York Public Library, where I found Mr. X waiting for me with a coffee of his own. He rose and smiled as I neared his table.

After exchanging pleasantries and updating each other on goings on with each of our families for a few minutes, we got into the matter at hand.

Luke: Our prior conversations have been helpful in supplying context to how the global financial system has evolved into its current state, but I'm left wondering how you think all of this ends? Where are we going from here?

Mr. X: Have you ever heard of the "Triffin Dilemma"?

Luke: Of course.

Mr. X: Do you know the full history of it?

Luke: I think so, but can you remind me just in case I have some of the details wrong?

Mr. X: Robert Triffin coined the term and the problem it describes in 1959, but it didn't become popular until the late 1960s when Robert Triffin began referring to it, and hence, it was named for him. The Triffin Dilemma, in essence, says that if one nation uses its currency as the reserve currency for the world, it must run ever-growing deficits to supply the currency needed for the global economy. Ultimately, these deficits drive such a significant hollowing out of domestic productive assets that foreign creditors of the issuing nation begin to question the issuing nation's ability to repay sovereign debt in real terms.

Luke: Okay, go on…

Mr. X: Well, no one wants to admit it, but we're there. We arrived there in 2008, and we have spent the last decade muddling along. The BIS always knew this day would come as well, as I noted in Jelle Zijlstra's comments during one of prior get-togethers.

Luke: If we've muddled along for the last ten years, why can't we keep muddling along for another five or ten years?

Mr. X: Remember our prior discussion—Demographics, Debt, Geology, Economic Reality, and the Repeated Weaponization of the USD are five different forcing functions all pushing us in the same direction—they make another five- or ten-year muddle-through period mathematically highly unlikely.

Luke: So how do you think this will end?

Mr. X: What I have described to you in these past few meetings has at its core been this: Nations can no longer afford to stockpile USDs/USTs ad infinitum as their primary reserve asset. As I noted before, it is a redline for certain creditor nations around the world, and in particular China, Russia, and certain OPEC nations.

Luke: So how will this end?

Mr. X: Luke, you are too young to remember this, but I am not. This has all happened before.

Luke: What's happened before?

Mr. X: US creditors are dictating US foreign policy by cutting off official foreign funding to the United States.

Luke: Wait, what? When did that happen?

Mr. X: It last happened in the late 1960s.... Let me read something to you:

[He opened his folder, and showing he was well-prepared as always, he pulled out a sheet of paper and began to read from it.]

> Millions of Americans heard President Johnson say in his startling television speech on March 31 [1968] that he would not substantially escalate the Vietnam War, but few heard the peremptory voice of gold speaking in the background. In the past, the military compulsion of the Tet defeat would have sent many thousands of fresh troops to Vietnam to meet the new challenge. But that was before the US gold crisis.

One expert noted: "*The European financiers are forcing peace on us. For the first time in American history, our European creditors have forced the resignation of an American President.*" (*Wall Street Journal*, April 4, 1968).

Until 1968, Europe had, in an important respect, borne the major cost of supporting world confidence that America's overseas military expenditures would not impair the value of America's currency. *Europe did this by holding onto the dollars thrown off by these expenditures rather than cashing them in for US gold.* The Europeans had protested since 1964 against absorbing these dollars, and finally, with the gold crisis, they drew the line against continuing thus to finance US military policy.

America was left to pay the costs itself, but they were beyond its means. And at that point it became clear that the US could not continue its current rate of overseas military spending—much less increase it—without bringing on a complete collapse of confidence in its currency.

[Source: "Sieve of Gold," *Rampart Magazine*, May 1968

http://www.gata.org/files/RampartsMay1968-SieveOfGold.pdf. Emphasis mine]

Before I comment on that, let me read you one more passage—an interview with Marriner Eccles, former chairman of the Federal Reserve Board, in *Forbes Magazine*, as quoted in May 1968 *Ramparts Magazine*.

Marriner Eccles: Just list some of our national problems—the very large and continuing budget deficit, the inflationary pressures, the balance-of-payments deficit, the lack of confidence in our dollar, the riots in our cities, the unrest on our campuses, the split among all classes of our populace and within our political parties. I believe that all of these can be traced to a common cause.

Forbes: Which is?

Eccles: Which is the war in Vietnam.

Mr. X: …and it's happening again. For example, during a public speaking appearance on October 8, 2014 that was later published on YouTube, Lawrence Wilkerson, the former Chief of Staff to Secretary of State Colin Powell, was asked:

> **Are there any consequences to the US continuously racking up debt? How do you see that playing out?**

> **Wilkerson:** That's an excellent question and it's my greatest fear. Yes, there are dire consequences.

> If you've listened to some of the people that have gone public lately, one of them went viral on the Internet, I'm not sure how much to believe him though. He's one of the principal advisors to what the CIA calls its Futures Project, where it does a report for 2025, and 2030 and so on, it looks out to the future.

> That's not just the CIA, it's the DNI now under the National Intelligence Council, which is really the whole intelligence community feeding into that, feeding into the NIC. He says that what he sees around the world, and he's told the intelligence community this, and they're now using their very sophisticated assets to measure this, and I know they're sophisticated, I've used them, with them, against North Korea principally, to see if what he's saying is true.

> That is to say that gold is being moved in sort of unique ways, concentrated and secret and unique ways, and capitals are slowly but surely and methodically divesting

themselves of US Treasuries. That Beijing and Moscow are both complicit in this, and that what they're trying to do is weaken the dollar.

So what you see right now in the supposed strengthening of the dollar is really a false impression. What they want to do is what we did essentially when we abandoned the gold standard and then oil really became the standard because oil is demarcated and sold in dollars principally.

What they want to do is use Putin and others' oil power, petrodollars if you will, and I say that petro-yuan, petro-renminbi, petro-euro, whatever, to force the United States to lose its incredibly powerful role of owning the world's transactional action reserve currency.

If that happens, a similar thing will happen to what Dwight Eisenhower threatened the British with, in the IMF, when it invaded Suez with the French and Israelis. The real powerful move that Ike made was to threaten a run on the [British] pound. Eden had to back off, he had to back off. He couldn't take that.

So what we're looking at is the possible use by others in the world of our dependence on the dollar to give us so much power that we otherwise would not have…. Charles de Gaulle once said it was vicious what we did after the war when we had the world's reserve currency…and take that power away from us.

And the [US Federal] debt increases *enormously* the capability [of these other nations] to do that. And the debt is staggering, if you think about it. If you just look at it and understand what the Fed's been doing in terms of Quantitative Easing and just printing more and more money. The only reason you can do that is because you own the world's transactional reserve currency.

You can print money and money and money and you don't do what Mbutu did for example, drive inflation up to 300,000 percent. Or, for example, what the Germans had happen to them in the 1920s; you know the old adage of pushing a wheelbarrow full of marks in order to buy a loaf of bread.

Could it get that bad in the American Empire? Yes, it could. Especially if the rest of the world decides that's a good thing to do and goes along with it. Or decides that it has to do it, it has to use Euros or Yen, or let's just call on SDRs at the IMF, something the Chinese kind of like.

Could you create something other than a currency to be that to which everyone goes in a crisis? Yes you could. SDRs would be just that, at the IMF or wherever they might reside.

[https://www.youtube.com/watch?v=YM_MH_Bfq5c. Quote begins at 47:45.]

And contrary to what many think, what some have called "the de-dollarization of global energy markets" has been accelerating meaningfully since mid-2014. Former senior level CIA analyst Charles Duelfer echoed some of Wilkerson's sentiments. Let me read them to you:

American media seems to be focused on domestic affairs while astonishing things are going beyond the borders— and we seem to stand by watching helplessly. The United States position of prominence is eroding.

Yesterday, at a summit in Shanghai between China's President Xi Jinping and Russian President Vladimir Putin a massive 30-year natural gas deal was signed to provide Russian gas to China. The agreement has been under negotiation for years and its fruition is a big deal for energy markets and international politics.

Less noticed, but possibly even more interesting, was an agreement between Russia and China aimed at undermining the role of the US dollar as the base currency. The Russian bank VTB and the Bank of China signed an agreement in the presence of Xi and Putin to avoid using the dollar and conduct exchanges in domestic currencies. This is a really big signal. The all mighty dollar may not always be all mighty.

Look at the world (or even just the United States) from the position of China. What makes America a super power? Is it the military? Partly. Is it nuclear weapons? Not so much. What really gives us leverage is the position of the dollar as the base currency. In the last financial crisis, we escaped largely by printing money. Other countries can't get away with that without causing massive inflation.

Sitting in Beijing, it could be seen as a financial attack—US Treasury printing tons of dollars that has the effect of exporting inflation to other countries. We borrow money (by selling treasuries to finance our wars, debt, TARP, etc.) and then pay them off by, in essence, printing dollars.

The role of the dollar as base currency is a uniquely powerful lever. It is one that is rarely thought of in terms of national security, but nothing is more important. If we lose it, we will have lost our position as the last super power. Period.

Beijing, Moscow, and others are well aware of this. The role of the dollar also gives us the currently valuable tool of sanctions. If Washington decides to limit banking use of dollars for transactions with certain entities, e.g., in Russia or Iran, then we can impose our will on the international financial system. You can bet there is no higher strategic priority than to undermine that position.

We are blindly squandering this leverage from inattention and by our inability to control our appetite for printed dollars. This is a national security issue, not just a budget issue.

[American Vulnerability – The Dollar: Charles Duelfer - May 22, 2014

http://www.charlesduelfer.com/blog/?p=239]

Luke: Wow…so what does this mean for the US?

Mr. X: Well, similar to how not stockpiling USD/USTs anymore is a redline for China, Russia, and other global creditor nations, the US government cannot afford for the world no longer to stockpile USDs/USTs ad infinitum as its primary reserve asset—it is a redline for the American government. That suggests there will be one of two outcomes.

Luke: Which are what?

Mr. X: A really positive one (that may cause some near-term disruption) or a really negative one.

Luke: What's the really positive outcome?

Mr. X: A systemic restructuring of the global currency system that ends up significantly reducing the USD's role as primary global reserve currency, effectively devaluing the USD against some sort of neutral asset—gold, or perhaps SDRs—or that devalues SDRs in gold and, thereby, devalues all currencies in favor of gold.

Luke: What's the really negative outcome?

Mr. X: World War III where the United States fights China and Russia, as Graham Allison has begun to discuss as a risk in his book *Thucydides' Trap*.

Luke: Yikes…which do you think will happen?

Mr. X: As I mentioned earlier, Winston Churchill once said that "The Americans always do the right thing, after they've tried everything else." I think that is still true, and the US has been fruitfully trying everything else for at least a decade. I'm optimistic that it will do the right thing this time, and importantly, so are some important Russian advisors to Putin. Remember that article I quoted before from the *Independent?*

[Mr. X dug in his folder for a moment until he pulled out the article.]

Trump victory averted World War 3, top Putin aide Glaziev claims – 11/11/16

One of Vladimir Putin's closest advisors has claimed Donald Trump's victory has averted a third world war.

Speaking after Mr Trump won a shock victory over Hillary Clinton on Tuesday, Kremlin advisor Sergei Glaziev said the Democrat politician was a "symbol of war" and under Mr. Trump the US had "a chance to change course."

He told Russian news wire RNS: "Americans had two choices: World War Three or multilateral peace.

"Clinton was a symbol of war, and Trump has a chance to change this course."

[http://www.independent.co.uk/news/world/americas/us-elections/world-war-three-donald-trump-president-averted-putin-aide-claims-a7412111.html]

Luke: So what are the United States' options if it is to avoid World War III?

Mr. X: They are fairly straightforward. Once another nation gains the ability to print its own currency for oil as it appears China has, there are three possible outcomes for the US:

1. **Slash US government spending to maintain the value of the USD:** Rising healthcare premiums under ACA and falling US infrastructure spending are symptoms that this has been tried, but at ~22% of US GDP, the US cannot slash US Federal spending without counterproductively crashing both the US economy and US Federal tax receipts (thereby widening the deficit.)
   [Here Mr. X referred me to a chart on public-construction spending.]
2. **Have the Fed print all the "helicopter money" needed to fund US Federal deficits:** This would be negative for the USD, and was frowned upon as a strategy by the BIS in a white paper from late 2016.
3. **Devalue/weaken the USD significantly,** thereby increasing US tax receipts and rebalancing the US economy away from consumption toward production, centered around US energy and alternative energy sectors and infrastructure as US energy costs rise.

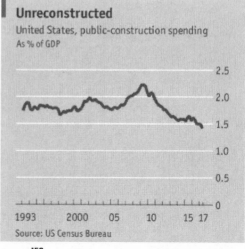

Unreconstructed
United States, public-construction spending
As % of GDP

Source: US Census Bureau

As I noted before, the first option has been tried, but it became counterproductive once US deficits began widening in the third

150

quarter of 2016. [Here he referred to a chart showing the US deficit as a percentage of the US GDP from 1969-2016.] The second option was frowned upon by the BIS in the same quarter after Ben Bernanke began writing some articles floating helicopter money trial balloons...leaving only the third option, in my opinion.

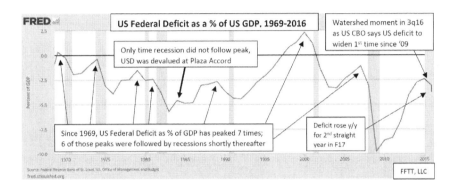

Luke: A major USD devaluation occurring through a systemic restructuring would likely have tectonic implications for investment returns, no?

Mr. X: Yes, and in my eyes, it appears that many of the usual suspects are once again positioned to get run over by this trend— retirees, commercial banks, pensions—all holding USTs and other low-rate fixed rate debt for "safety," not realizing what Warren Buffett said about fixed rate debt five years ago.

Luke: For the benefit of our readers, can you remind me again what that was?

Mr. X: Sure—it's this... [He pulled out a sheet of paper containing a quote from 2012 by Warren Buffet.]

Most of these currency-based investments are thought of as "safe." In truth, they are among the most dangerous of assets...their risk is huge.

"In God We Trust" may be imprinted on our currency, but the hand that activates our government's printing press has been all too human. High interest rates, of course, can compensate purchasers for the inflation risk they face with currency-based investments—and indeed, rates in the early 1980s did that job nicely. Current rates, however, do not come close to offsetting the purchasing-power risk that investors assume. Right now, bonds should come with a warning label.

Luke: My goodness...

Mr. X: Yes. This is why I reached out to you—given your ability to put the pieces together, hopefully, people will read your book, see what is happening and protect themselves from what appears likely to happen, indeed what *must* happen to avoid a much worse outcome.

Luke: Which is what, to summarize?

Mr. X: The real value of fixed rate sovereign debt must be significantly eroded away by inflation in other asset classes.

Luke: Makes perfect sense to me, and I agree with you. I will get busy writing...Thank you for sharing your insights. I am forever indebted, Mr. X.

Mr. X: You're welcome, and thank you. I look forward to seeing the final product.

ABOUT THE AUTHOR

Luke Gromen began his career in the mid-1990s in the Research Department at Midwest Research before moving over to institutional equity sales and becoming a partner. While in sales, Luke was a founding editor of Midwest's widely-read weekly summary, *Heard in the Midwest,* for the firm's clients, in which he aggregated and combined proprietary research from Midwest with inputs from other sources.

In 2006, Luke left FTN Midwest to become a founding partner of Cleveland Research Company. At CRC, Luke continued to work in sales and edit CRC's flagship weekly research summary piece, *Straight from the Source,* for the firm's customers.

In 2014, Luke left Cleveland Research to found FFTT, LLC ("Forest for the Trees"), a macro/thematic research firm catering to institutions and sophisticated individuals that aggregates a wide variety of macroeconomic, thematic, and sector trends in an unconventional manner to identify investable developing economic bottlenecks for his customers; he has found that excess investment returns tend to accrue to economic bottlenecks over time.

Luke's vision for FFTT was to create a firm that would address the opportunity he saw created by applying what customers and former colleagues consistently described as a "unique ability to put the big picture pieces together" during a time when he saw an increasing "silo-ing" of perspectives occurring on Wall Street and in corporate America.

Luke Gromen is a graduate of the University of Cincinnati and received his MBA from Case Western Reserve University. He earned the CFA designation in 2003.

GET INSIDE THE RING

SUBSCRIBE TO FFTT TREE RINGS

Now, the increasing commoditization of data means it's the **interpretation** *of that data that provides the advantage in investment markets.*

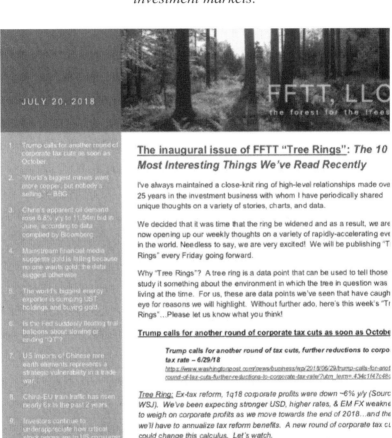

JULY 20, 2018

FFTT, LLC
the forest for the trees

1. Trump calls for another round of corporate tax cuts as soon as October

2. "World's biggest miners want more copper, but nobody's selling" – BBG

3. China's apparent oil demand rose 6.8% y/y to 11.54m b/d in June, according to data compiled by Bloomberg

4. Mainstream financial media suggests gold is falling because no one wants gold; the data suggest otherwise

5. The world's biggest energy exporter is dumping UST holdings and buying gold

6. Is the Fed suddenly floating trial balloons about slowing or ending "QT"?

7. US imports of Chinese rare earth elements represents a strategic vulnerability in a trade war

8. China-EU train traffic has risen nearly 6x in the past 2 years

9. Investors continue to underappreciate how critical stock prices are to US consumer spending, tax receipts

10. A recently-released RAND study suggests Chinese military capabilities are rapidly closing the gap with the US

The inaugural issue of FFTT "Tree Rings": *The 10 Most Interesting Things We've Read Recently*

I've always maintained a close-knit ring of high-level relationships made over 25 years in the investment business with whom I have periodically shared unique thoughts on a variety of stories, charts, and data.

We decided that it was time that the ring be widened and as a result, we are now opening up our weekly thoughts on a variety of rapidly-accelerating eve in the world. Needless to say, we are very excited! We will be publishing "T Rings" every Friday going forward.

Why "Tree Rings"? A tree ring is a data point that can be used to tell those study it something about the environment in which the tree in question was living at the time. For us, these are data points we've seen that have caugh eye for reasons we will highlight. Without further ado, here's this week's "Tr Rings"...Please let us know what you think!

Trump calls for another round of corporate tax cuts as soon as Octobe

> *Trump calls for another round of tax cuts, further reductions to corpo tax rate – 6/29/18*
> https://www.washingtonpost.com/news/business/wp/2018/06/29/trump-calls-for-anot round-of-tax-cuts-further-reductions-to-corporate-tax-rate/?utm_term=.434c1f47c48c

> *Tree Ring:* Ex-tax reform, 1q18 corporate profits were down ~6% y/y (Sourc WSJ). We've been expecting stronger USD, higher rates, & EM FX weakne to weigh on corporate profits as we move towards the end of 2018…and the we'll have to annualize tax reform benefits. A new round of corporate tax ct could change this calculus. Let's watch.

"World's biggest miners want more copper, but nobody's selling" -BB

> *World's biggest miners want more copper but nobody's selling – 7/16*
> https://www.bloomberg.com/news/articles/2018-07-15/the-world-s-biggest-miners-wi more-copper-but-nobody-s-selling

In an economic landscape where events are changing rapidly and information is plentiful, it's easy to get overloaded. Getting concise analysis of the most impactful information will positively impact your investment process.

Before Luke Gromen left his Wall Street career to begin Forest for the Trees (FFTT, LLC), he began seeing a gap in the way information was being disseminated and interpreted that was leading to an increasing "silo-ing" of investment perspectives.

Data was increasingly becoming commoditized, while connecting the dots and value-added interpretation of the data seemed to be becoming rarer and rarer; people were often "missing the forest for the trees" because the dots were not being connected.

Luke began FFTT for that very reason. He has been in this business since 1995—a long time. In his prior roles as a Wall Street salesperson and analyst, he created and edited a weekly report that highlighted ten key points of interest he thought would be most helpful to his clients' investing process. He called it "The 10 Most Interesting Things I've Seen This Week." Although he admits it wasn't a very creative title, his customers *loved* it.

When Luke stepped out on his own in 2014 to form FFTT, he did so to provide unique, independent, value-added contrarian thinking to sophisticated investors. Unfortunately, "The 10 Most Interesting Things" weekly report got shelved as he began building FFTT from scratch.

Four years later, he decided it was time to bring "The 10 Most Interesting Things" back into circulation. He's breathed new life and depth into it, and now it has become "FFTT Tree Rings."

"FFTT Tree Rings" is an annual subscription that offers Luke's weekly insights. Each weekly report consists of a series of ten stories and charts he's found interesting. Each story has a brief analysis highlighting why it is potentially impactful to investors' outlooks.

The investment for an annual subscription to "FFTT Tree Rings" is $96/year. To subscribe, visit:

https://fftt-llc.com/index.php/subscribe-to-fftt/treerings

Here's what some of our FFTT Tree Rings Clients have to say:

"Tree Rings' is something I'll be looking forward to every Friday. Always good to read what another has concluded upon reading the articles I so often have put aside. Your highlights are concise, thought-provoking, a view from a different window so to speak...just what I like to see."

— J.H.

"Luke, thank you, really what you promised: short and on point. Love it."

— S.B.

"I'm digesting as much as I can from your tweets. Your research is brilliant and every individual investor needs your insights. Just signed up. Absolutely brilliant! This is one of the best insights I have ever come across."

— G.M.

"Just wanted to send a quick note to say that I'm really enjoying 'Tree Rings' and find it to be an awesome value! I've been following your work since I saw you on *Real Vision* the first time. I feel really fortunate to have found your work."

— S.M.

Check out a sample of FFTT Tree Rings at https://fftt-llc.com/images/tree-rings-7-20-18.pdf.

In the aftermath of the 2008 financial crisis, it has become increasingly important to understand not just economics, but political economics. The failure to understand critical aspects of political economy has caused many investors either significant actual losses or significant opportunity cost losses on their investments.

The unipolar world that existed from the time the USSR collapsed in 1989 until a few years ago is now ending; in its place, a more multipolar world is rapidly emerging. If you are not factoring these changes into your economic analysis, you are investing with a big blind spot. Our unique ability to identify and analyze political economic and geopolitical factors *and* how those factors impact your investment process are a key reason FFTT has thrived in the five years since its founding.

Luke has always maintained a very small ring of high-level relationships made over twenty-five years, with whom he has shared unique thoughts on stories, charts, and data.

Now he has decided it is time the ring be widened, and he wants to open up his thoughts to a whole new audience interested in his perspectives on rapidly-accelerating events in the world.

Get inside the ring and connect the dots to see the bigger picture.

Have more questions? Please check out FAQS at https://fftt-llc.com/index.php/subscribe-to-fftt/tree-rings-faq.

Ready to get inside the ring? Visit https://fftt-llc.com/index.php/subscribe-to-fftt/treerings to subscribe.

Made in the USA
Columbia, SC
03 October 2020